Scaling Big Data with Hadoop and Solr

Second Edition

Understand, design, build, and optimize your big data search engine with Hadoop and Apache Solr

Hrishikesh Vijay Karambelkar

BIRMINGHAM - MUMBAI

Scaling Big Data with Hadoop and Solr
Second Edition

Copyright © 2015 Packt Publishing

All rights reserved. No part of this book may be reproduced, stored in a retrieval system, or transmitted in any form or by any means, without the prior written permission of the publisher, except in the case of brief quotations embedded in critical articles or reviews.

Every effort has been made in the preparation of this book to ensure the accuracy of the information presented. However, the information contained in this book is sold without warranty, either express or implied. Neither the author, nor Packt Publishing, and its dealers and distributors will be held liable for any damages caused or alleged to be caused directly or indirectly by this book.

Packt Publishing has endeavored to provide trademark information about all of the companies and products mentioned in this book by the appropriate use of capitals. However, Packt Publishing cannot guarantee the accuracy of this information.

First published: August 2013

Second edition: April 2015

Production reference: 1230415

Published by Packt Publishing Ltd.
Livery Place
35 Livery Street
Birmingham B3 2PB, UK.

ISBN 978-1-78355-339-6

www.packtpub.com

Credits

Author
Hrishikesh Vijay Karambelkar

Reviewers
Ramzi Alqrainy
Walt Stoneburner
Ning Sun
Ruben Teijeiro

Commissioning Editor
Kartikey Pandey

Acquisition Editor
Nikhil Chinnari
Reshma Raman

Content Development Editor
Susmita Sabat

Technical Editor
Aman Preet Singh

Copy Editors
Sonia Cheema
Tani Kothari

Project Coordinator
Milton Dsouza

Proofreader
Simran Bhogal
Safis Editing

Indexer
Mariammal Chettiyar

Production Coordinator
Arvindkumar Gupta

Cover Work
Arvindkumar Gupta

About the Author

Hrishikesh Vijay Karambelkar is an enterprise architect who has been developing a blend of technical and entrepreneurial experience for more than 14 years. His core expertise lies in working on multiple subjects, which include big data, enterprise search, semantic web, link data analysis, analytics, and he also enjoys architecting solutions for the next generation of product development for IT organizations. He spends most of his time at work, solving challenging problems faced by the software industry. Currently, he is working as the Director of Data Capabilities at The Digital Group.

In the past, Hrishikesh has worked in the domain of graph databases; some of his work has been published at international conferences, such as VLDB, ICDE, and others. He has also written *Scaling Apache Solr*, published by *Packt Publishing*. He enjoys travelling, trekking, and taking pictures of birds living in the dense forests of India. He can be reached at `http://hrishikesh.karambelkar.co.in/`.

> I am thankful to all my reviewers who have helped me organize this book especially Susmita from Packt Publishing for her consistent follow-ups. I would like to thank my dear wife, Dhanashree, for her constant support and encouragement during the course of writing this book.

About the Reviewers

Ramzi Alqrainy is one of the most well-recognized experts in the Middle East in the fields of artificial intelligence and information retrieval. He's an active researcher and technology blogger who specializes in information retrieval.

Ramzi is currently resolving complex search issues in and around the Lucene/Solr ecosystem at Lucidworks. He also manages the search and reporting functions at OpenSooq, where he capitalizes on the solid experience he's gained in open source technologies to scale up the search engine and supportive systems there.

His experience in Solr, ElasticSearch, Mahout, and the Hadoop stack have contributed directly to business growth through their implementation. He also did projects that helped key people at OpenSooq slice and dice information easily through dashboards and data visualization solutions.

Besides the development of more than eight full-stack search engines, Ramzi was also able to solve many complicated challenges that dealt with agglutination and stemming in the Arabic language.

He holds a master's degree in computer science, was among the top 1 percent in his class, and was part of the honor roll.

Ramzi can be reached at `http://ramzialqrainy.com`. His LinkedIn profile can be found at `http://www.linkedin.com/in/ramzialqrainy`. You can reach him through his e-mail address, which is `ramzi.alqrainy@gmail.com`.

Walt Stoneburner is a software architect and engineer with over 30 years of commercial application development and consulting experience. He holds a degree in computer science and statistics and is currently the CTO for Emperitas Services Group (http://emperitas.com/), where he designs predictive analytical and modeling software tools for statisticians, economists, and customers. Emperitas shows you where to spend your marketing dollars most effectively, how to target messages to specific demographics, and how to quantify the hidden decision-making process behind customer psychology and buying habits.

He has also been heavily involved in quality assurance, configuration management, and security. His interests include programming language designs, collaborative and multiuser applications, big data, knowledge management, mobile applications, data visualization, and even ASCII art.

Self-described as a closet geek, Walt also evaluates software products and consumer electronics, draws comics (NapkinComics.com), runs a freelance photography studio that specializes in portraits (CharismaticMoments.com), writes humor pieces, performs sleight of hand, enjoys game mechanic design, and can occasionally be found on ham radio or tinkering with gadgets.

Walt may be reached directly via e-mail at wls@wwco.com or Walt.Stoneburner@ gmail.com.

He publishes a tech and humor blog called the Walt-O-Matic at http://www. wwco.com/~wls/blog/ and is pretty active on social media sites, especially the experimental ones.

Some more of his book reviews and contributions include:

- *Anti-Patterns and Patterns in Software Configuration Management* by *William J. Brown, Hays W. McCormick*, and *Scott W. Thomas*, published by Wiley
- *Exploiting Software: How to Break Code* by *Greg Hoglund*, published by Addison-Wesley Professional
- *Ruby on Rails Web Mashup Projects* by *Chang Sau Sheong*, published by Packt Publishing
- *Building Dynamic Web 2.0 Websites with Ruby on Rails* by *A P Rajshekhar*, published by Packt Publishing
- *Instant Sinatra Starter* by *Joe Yates* published by Packt Publishing
- *C++ Multithreading Cookbook* by *Miloš Ljumović*, published by Packt Publishing

- *Learning Selenium Testing Tools with Python* by *Unmesh Gundecha*, published by Packt Publishing
- *Trapped in Whittier (A Trent Walker Thriller Book 1)* by *Michael W. Layne*, published by Amazon Digital South Asia Services, Inc
- *South Mouth: Hillbilly Wisdom, Redneck Observations & Good Ol' Boy Logic* by *Cooter Brown* and *Walt Stoneburner*, published by CreateSpace Independent Publishing Platform

Ning Sun is a software engineer currently working for LeanCloud, a Chinese start-up, which provides a one-stop Backend-as-a-Service for mobile apps. Being a start-up engineer, he has to come up with solutions for various kinds of problems and play different roles. In spite of this, he has always been an enthusiast of open source technology. He has contributed to several open source projects and learned a lot from them.

Ning worked on Delicious.com in 2013, which was one of the most important websites in the Web 2.0 era. The search function of Delicious is powered by Solr Cluster and it might be one of the largest-ever deployments of Solr.

He was a reviewer for another Solr book, called *Apache Solr Cookbook*, published by Packt Publishing.

You can always find Ning at `https://github.com/sunng87` and on Twitter at `@Sunng`.

Ruben Teijeiro is an active contributor to the Drupal community, a speaker at conferences around Europe, and a mentor in code sprints, where he helps initiate people to contribute to an open source project, such as Drupal. He defines himself as a Drupal Hero.

After 2 years of working for Ericsson in Sweden, he has been employed by Tieto, where he combines Drupal with different technologies to create complex software solutions.

He has loved different kinds of technologies since he started to program in QBasic with his first MSX computer when he was about 10. You can find more about him on his drupal.org profile (`http://dgo.to/@rteijeiro`) and his personal blog (`http://drewpull.com`).

I would like to thank my parents since they helped me develop my love for computers and pushed me to learn programming. I am the person I've become today solely because of them.

I would also like to thank my beautiful wife, Ana, who has stood beside me throughout my career and been my constant companion in this adventure.

---

www.PacktPub.com

Support files, eBooks, discount offers, and more

For support files and downloads related to your book, please visit www.PacktPub.com.

Did you know that Packt offers eBook versions of every book published, with PDF and ePub files available? You can upgrade to the eBook version at www.PacktPub.com and as a print book customer, you are entitled to a discount on the eBook copy. Get in touch with us at service@packtpub.com for more details.

At www.PacktPub.com, you can also read a collection of free technical articles, sign up for a range of free newsletters and receive exclusive discounts and offers on Packt books and eBooks.

https://www2.packtpub.com/books/subscription/packtlib

Do you need instant solutions to your IT questions? PacktLib is Packt's online digital book library. Here, you can search, access, and read Packt's entire library of books.

Why subscribe?

- Fully searchable across every book published by Packt
- Copy and paste, print, and bookmark content
- On demand and accessible via a web browser

Free access for Packt account holders

If you have an account with Packt at www.PacktPub.com, you can use this to access PacktLib today and view 9 entirely free books. Simply use your login credentials for immediate access.

Table of Contents

Preface	**v**
Chapter 1: Processing Big Data Using Hadoop and MapReduce	**1**
Apache Hadoop's ecosystem	**2**
Core components	4
Understanding Hadoop's ecosystem	6
Configuring Apache Hadoop	**8**
Prerequisites	9
Setting up ssh without passphrase	10
Configuring Hadoop	11
Running Hadoop	**14**
Setting up a Hadoop cluster	**17**
Common problems and their solutions	**19**
Summary	**20**
Chapter 2: Understanding Apache Solr	**21**
Setting up Apache Solr	**22**
Prerequisites for setting up Apache Solr	22
Running Apache Solr on jetty	23
Running Solr on other J2EE containers	25
Hello World with Apache Solr!	25
Understanding Solr administration	27
Solr navigation	27
Common problems and solutions	28
The Apache Solr architecture	**29**
Configuring Solr	**31**
Understanding the Solr structure	32
Defining the Solr schema	32
Solr fields	33
Dynamic fields in Solr	34
Copying the fields	35

[i]

Table of Contents

Dealing with field types	35
Additional metadata configuration	36
Other important elements of the Solr schema	37
Configuration files of Apache Solr	37
Working with solr.xml and Solr core	38
Instance configuration with solrconfig.xml	38
Understanding the Solr plugin	40
Other configuration	41
Loading data in Apache Solr	**42**
Extracting request handler – Solr Cell	42
Understanding data import handlers	43
Interacting with Solr through SolrJ	44
Working with rich documents (Apache Tika)	46
Querying for information in Solr	**47**
Summary	**48**
Chapter 3: Enabling Distributed Search using Apache Solr	**49**
Understanding a distributed search	**50**
Distributed search patterns	50
Apache Solr and distributed search	52
Working with SolrCloud	**53**
Why ZooKeeper?	53
The SolrCloud architecture	54
Building an enterprise distributed search using SolrCloud	57
Setting up SolrCloud for development	58
Setting up SolrCloud for production	60
Adding a document to SolrCloud	64
Creating shards, collections, and replicas in SolrCloud	65
Common problems and resolutions	66
Sharding algorithm and fault tolerance	**68**
Document Routing and Sharding	68
Shard splitting	70
Load balancing and fault tolerance in SolrCloud	71
Apache Solr and Big Data – integration with MongoDB	**72**
What is NoSQL and how is it related to Big Data?	73
MongoDB at glance	73
Installing MongoDB	75
Creating Solr indexes from MongoDB	77
Summary	**79**
Chapter 4: Big Data Search Using Hadoop and Its Ecosystem	**81**
Understanding NoSQL	**82**
Working with the Solr HDFS connector	**82**

Big data search using Katta	**86**
How Katta works?	86
Setting up the Katta cluster	87
Creating Katta indexes	88
Using Solr 1045 Patch – map-side indexing	**89**
Using Solr 1301 Patch – reduce-side indexing	**91**
Distributed search using Apache Blur	**93**
Setting up Apache Blur with Hadoop	94
Apache Solr and Cassandra	**96**
Working with Cassandra and Solr	98
Single node configuration	98
Integrating with multinode Cassandra	100
Scaling Solr through Storm	**101**
Getting along with Apache Storm	102
Advanced analytics with Solr	**104**
Integrating Solr and R	105
Summary	**107**
Chapter 5: Scaling Search Performance	**109**
Understanding the limits	**110**
Optimizing search schema	**111**
Specifying default search field	111
Configuring search schema fields	111
Stop words	112
Stemming	112
Index optimization	**114**
Limiting indexing buffer size	115
When to commit changes?	115
Optimizing index merge	117
Optimize option for index merging	118
Optimizing the container	119
Optimizing concurrent clients	119
Optimizing Java virtual memory	120
Optimizing search runtime	**121**
Optimizing through search query	122
Filter queries	122
Optimizing the Solr cache	122
The filter cache	124
The query result cache	124
The document cache	124
The field value cache	124
The lazy field loading	125
Optimizing Hadoop	125

[iii]

Monitoring Solr instance	**128**
Using SolrMeter	130
Summary	**131**
Appendix: Use Cases for Big Data Search	**133**
E-Commerce websites	**133**
Log management for banking	**134**
The problem	134
How can it be tackled?	135
High-level design	136
Index	**139**

Preface

With the growth of information assets in enterprises, the need to build a rich, scalable search application that can handle a lot of data has becomes critical. Today, Apache Solr is one of the most widely adapted, scalable, feature-rich, and best performing open source search application servers. Similarly, Apache Hadoop is one of the most popular Big Data platforms and is widely preferred by many organizations to store and process large datasets.

Scaling Big Data with Hadoop and Solr, Second Edition is intended to help its readers build a high performance Big Data enterprise search engine with the help of Hadoop and Solr. This starts with a basic understanding of Hadoop and Solr, and gradually develops into building an efficient, scalable enterprise search repository for Big Data, using various techniques throughout the practical chapters.

What this book covers

Chapter 1, Processing Big Data Using Hadoop and MapReduce, introduces you to Apache Hadoop and its ecosystem, HDFS and MapReduce. You will also learn how to write MapReduce programs, configure Hadoop clusters, configuration files, and administrate your cluster.

Chapter 2, Understanding Apache Solr, introduces you to Apache Solr. It explains how you can configure the Solr instance, how to create indexes and load your data in the Solr repository, and how you can use Solr effectively to search. It also discusses interesting features of Apache Solr.

Chapter 3, Enabling Distributed Search using Apache Solr, takes you through various aspects of enabling Solr for a distributed search, including with the use of SolrCloud. It also explains how Apache Solr and Big Data can come together to perform a scalable search.

Preface

Chapter 4, Big Data Search Using Hadoop and Its Ecosystem, explains the NoSQL and concepts of distributed search. It then explains how to use different algorithms for Big Data search, and includes covering shards and indexing. It also talks about integration with Cassandra, Apache Blur, Storm, and search analytics.

Chapter 5, Scaling Search Performance, will guide you in improving the performance of searches with Scaling Big Data. It covers different levels of optimization that you can perform on your Big Data search instance as the data keeps growing. It discusses different performance improvement techniques that can be implemented by users for the purposes of deployment.

Appendix, Use Cases for Big Data Search, discusses some of the most important business cases for high-level enterprise search architecture with Big Data and Solr.

What you need for this book

This book discusses different approaches; each approach needs a different set of software. Based on the requirements for building search applications, the respective software can be used. However, to run a minimal setup, you need the following software:

- JDK 1.8 and above
- Solr 4.10 and above
- Hadoop 2.5 and above

Who this book is for

Scaling Big Data with Hadoop and Solr, Second Edition provides step-by-step guidance for any user who intends to build high-performance, scalable, enterprise-ready search application servers. This book will appeal to developers, architects, and designers who wish to understand Apache Solr/Hadoop and its ecosystem, design an enterprise-ready application, and optimize it based on their requirements. This book enables you to build a scalable search without prior knowledge of Solr or Hadoop, with practical examples and case studies.

Conventions

In this book, you will find a number of styles of text that distinguish between different kinds of information. Here are some examples of these styles, and an explanation of their meaning.

[vi]

Preface

Code words in text, database table names, folder names, filenames, file extensions, pathnames, dummy URLs, user input, and Twitter handles are shown as follows: "By deleting the DFS data folder, you can find the location from hdfs-site.xml and restart the cluster."

A block of code is set as follows:

```
<configuration>
  <property>
    <name>fs.defaultFS</name>
    <value>hdfs://master-server:9000</value>
  </property>
</configuration>
```

Any command-line input or output is written as follows:

```
$ $HADOOP_PREFIX/sbin/mr-jobhistory-daemon.sh start historyserver
```

New terms and **important words** are shown in bold. Words that you see on the screen, in menus or dialog boxes for example, appear in the text like this: "You can validate the content created by your new MongoDB DIH by accessing the **Solr Admin** page, and running a query".

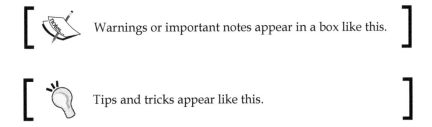

Warnings or important notes appear in a box like this.

Tips and tricks appear like this.

Reader feedback

Feedback from our readers is always welcome. Let us know what you think about this book—what you liked or may have disliked. Reader feedback is important for us to develop titles that you really get the most out of.

To send us general feedback, simply send an e-mail to feedback@packtpub.com, and mention the book title via the subject of your message.

If there is a topic that you have expertise in and you are interested in either writing or contributing to a book, see our author guide on www.packtpub.com/authors.

[vii]

Preface

Customer support

Now that you are the proud owner of a Packt book, we have a number of things to help you to get the most from your purchase.

Downloading the example code

You can download the example code files for all Packt books you have purchased from your account at http://www.packtpub.com. If you purchased this book elsewhere, you can visit http://www.packtpub.com/support and register to have the files e-mailed directly to you.

Errata

Although we have taken every care to ensure the accuracy of our content, mistakes do happen. If you find a mistake in one of our books—maybe a mistake in the text or the code—we would be grateful if you would report this to us. By doing so, you can save other readers from frustration and help us improve subsequent versions of this book. If you find any errata, please report them by visiting http://www.packtpub.com/submit-errata, selecting your book, clicking on the **errata submission form** link, and entering the details of your errata. Once your errata are verified, your submission will be accepted and the errata will be uploaded on our website, or added to any list of existing errata, under the Errata section of that title. Any existing errata can be viewed by selecting your title from http://www.packtpub.com/support.

Piracy

Piracy of copyright material on the Internet is an ongoing problem across all media. At Packt, we take the protection of our copyright and licenses very seriously. If you come across any illegal copies of our works, in any form, on the Internet, please provide us with the location address or website name immediately so that we can pursue a remedy.

Please contact us at copyright@packtpub.com with a link to the suspected pirated material.

We appreciate your help in protecting our authors, and our ability to bring you valuable content.

Questions

You can contact us at questions@packtpub.com if you are having a problem with any aspect of the book, and we will do our best to address it.

1
Processing Big Data Using Hadoop and MapReduce

Continuous evolution in computer sciences has enabled the world to work in a faster, more reliable, and more efficient manner. Many businesses have been transformed to utilize electronic media. They use information technologies to innovate the communication with their customers, partners, and suppliers. It has also given birth to new industries such as social media and e-commerce. This rapid increase in the amount of data has led to an "information explosion." To handle the problems of managing huge information, the computational capabilities have evolved too, with a focus on optimizing the hardware cost, giving rise to distributed systems. In today's world, this problem has multiplied; information is generated from disparate sources such as social media, sensors/embedded systems, and machine logs, in either a structured or an unstructured form. Processing of these large and complex data using traditional systems and methods is a challenging task. **Big Data** is an umbrella term that encompasses the management and processing of such data.

Big data is usually associated with high-volume and heavily growing data with unpredictable content. The IT advisory firm Gartner defines big data using 3Vs (high volume of data, high velocity of processing speed, and high variety of information). IBM has added a fourth V (high veracity) to this definition to make sure that the data is accurate and helps you make your business decisions. While the potential benefits of big data are real and significant, there remain many challenges. So, organizations that deal with such a high volumes of data, must work on the following areas:

- Data capture/acquisition from various sources
- Data massaging or curating
- Organization and storage

[1]

- Big data processing such as search, analysis, and querying
- Information sharing or consumption
- Information security and privacy

Big data poses a lot of challenges to the technologies in use today. Many organizations have started investing in these big data areas. As per Gartner, through 2015, 85% of the Fortune 500 organizations will be unable to exploit big data for a competitive advantage.

To handle the problem of storing and processing complex and large data, many software frameworks have been created to work on the big data problem. Among them, Apache Hadoop is one of the most widely used open source software frameworks for the storage and processing of big data. In this chapter, we are going to understand Apache Hadoop. We will be covering the following topics:

- Apache Hadoop's ecosystem
- Configuring Apache Hadoop
- Running Apache Hadoop
- Setting up a Hadoop cluster

Apache Hadoop's ecosystem

Apache Hadoop enables the distributed processing of large datasets across a commodity of clustered servers. It is designed to scale up from a single server to thousands of commodity hardware machines, each offering partial computational units and data storage.

The Apache Hadoop system comes with the following primary components:

- **Hadoop Distributed File System (HDFS)**
- MapReduce framework

The Apache Hadoop distributed file system or HDFS provides a file system that can be used to store data in a replicated and distributed manner across various nodes, which are part of the Hadoop cluster. Apache Hadoop provides a distributed data processing framework for large datasets by using a simple programming model called **MapReduce**.

Chapter 1

 A programming task that takes a set of data (key-value pair) and converts it into another set of data, is called **Map Task**. The results of map tasks are combined into one or many **Reduce Tasks**. Overall, this approach towards computing tasks is called the **MapReduce approach**.

The MapReduce programming paradigm forms the heart of the Apache Hadoop framework, and any application that is deployed on this framework must comply with MapReduce programming. The following figure demonstrates how MapReduce can be used to sort input documents with the MapReduce approach:

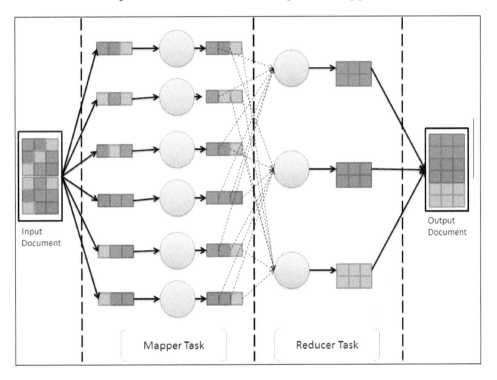

MapReduce can also be used to transform data from a domain into the corresponding range. We are going to look at these in more detail in the following chapters.

[3]

Processing Big Data Using Hadoop and MapReduce

Hadoop has been used in environments where data from various sources needs to be processed using large server farms. Hadoop is capable of running its cluster of nodes on commodity hardware, and does not demand any high-end server configuration. With this, Hadoop also brings scalability that enables administrators to add and remove nodes dynamically. Some of the most notable users of Hadoop are companies like Google (in the past), Facebook, and Yahoo, who process petabytes of data every day, and produce rich analytics to the consumer in the shortest possible time. All this is supported by a large community of users who consistently develop and enhance Hadoop every day. Apache Hadoop 2.0 onwards uses **YARN** (which stands for **Yet Another Resource Negotiator**).

> The Apache Hadoop 1.X MapReduce framework used concepts of job tracker and task tracker. If you are using the older Hadoop versions, it is recommended to move to Hadoop 2.x, which uses advanced MapReduce (also called 2.0). This was released in 2013.

Core components

The following diagram demonstrates how the core components of Apache Hadoop work together to ensure distributed exaction of user jobs:

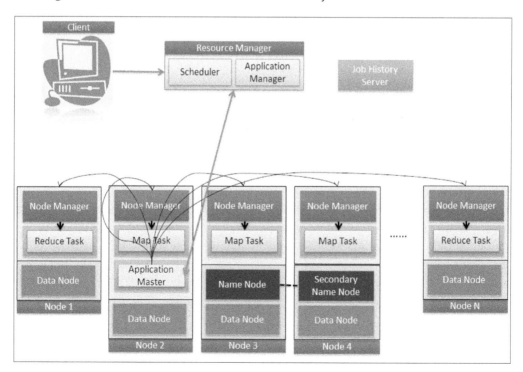

The **Resource Manager (RM)** in a Hadoop system is responsible for globally managing the resources of a cluster. Besides managing resources, it coordinates the allocation of resources on the cluster. RM consists of Scheduler and ApplicationsManager. As the names suggest, Scheduler provides resource allocation, whereas ApplicationsManager is responsible for client interactions (accepting jobs and identifying and assigning them to Application Masters).

The **Application Master (AM)** works for a complete application lifecycle, that is, the life of each MapReduce job. It interacts with RM to negotiate for resources.

The **Node Manager (NM)** is responsible for the management of all containers that run on a given node. It keeps a watch on resource usage (CPU, memory, and so on), and reports the resource health consistently to the resource manager.

All the metadata related to HDFS is stored on **NameNode**. The NameNode is the master node that performs coordination activities among data nodes, such as data replication across data nodes, naming system such as filenames, and the disk locations. NameNode stores the mapping of blocks on the Data Nodes. In a Hadoop cluster, there can only be one single *active* NameNode. NameNode regulates access to its file system with the use of HDFS-based APIs to create, open, edit, and delete HDFS files.

Earlier, NameNode, due to its functioning, was identified as the single point of failure in a Hadoop system. To compensate for this, the Hadoop framework introduced **SecondaryNameNode**, which constantly syncs with NameNode and can take over whenever NameNode is unavailable.

DataNodes are nothing but slaves that are deployed on all the nodes in a Hadoop cluster. DataNode is responsible for storing the application's data. Each uploaded data file in HDFS is split into multiple blocks, and these data blocks are stored on different data nodes. The default file block size in HDFS is 64 MB. Each Hadoop file block is mapped to two files in the data node; one file is the file block data, while the other is checksum.

When Hadoop is started, each DataNode connects to NameNode informing it of its availability to serve the requests. When the system is started, the namespace ID and software versions are verified by NameNode and DataNode sends the block report describing all the data blocks it holds for NameNode on startup. During runtime, each DataNode periodically sends a heartbeat signal to NameNode, confirming its availability. The default duration between two heartbeats is 3 seconds. NameNode assumes the unavailability of DataNode if it does not receive a heartbeat in 10 minutes by default; in which case, NameNode replicates the data blocks of that DataNode to other DataNodes.

When a client submits a job to Hadoop, the following activities take place:

1. Application manager launches AM to a given client job/application after negotiating with a specific node.
2. The AM, once booted, registers itself with the RM. All the client communication with AM happens through RM.
3. AM launches the container with help of NodeManager.
4. A container that is responsible for executing a MapReduce task reports the progress status to the AM through an application-specific protocol.
5. On receiving any request for data access on HDFS, NameNode takes the responsibility of returning to the nearest location of DataNode from its repository.

Understanding Hadoop's ecosystem

Although Hadoop provides excellent storage capabilities along with the MapReduce programming framework, it is still a challenging task to transform conventional programming into a MapReduce type of paradigm, as MapReduce is a completely different programming paradigm. The Hadoop ecosystem is designed to provide a set of rich applications and development framework. The following block diagram shows Apache Hadoop's ecosystem:

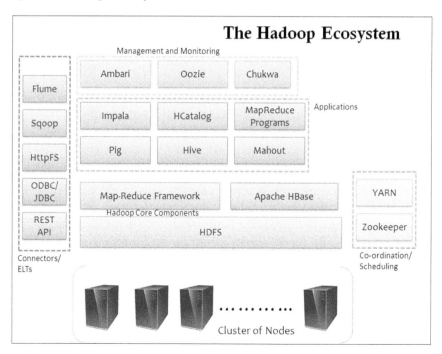

Chapter 1

We have already seen MapReduce, HDFS, and YARN. Let us look at each of the blocks.

HDFS is an append-only file system; it does not allow data modification. **Apache HBase** is a distributed, random-access, and column-oriented database. HBase directly runs on top of HDFS and allows application developers to read-write the HDFS data directly. HBase does not support SQL; hence, it is also called a **NoSQL** database. However, it provides a command line-based interface, as well as a rich set of APIs to update the data. The data in HBase gets stored as key-value pairs in HDFS.

Apache Pig provides another abstraction layer on top of MapReduce. It's a platform for the analysis of very large datasets that runs on HDFS. It also provides an infrastructure layer, consisting of a compiler that produces sequences of MapReduce programs, along with a language layer consisting of the query language Pig Latin. Pig was initially developed at Yahoo! Research to enable developers to create ad-hoc MapReduce jobs for Hadoop. Since then, many big organizations such as eBay, LinkedIn, and Twitter have started using Apache Pig.

Apache Hive provides data warehouse capabilities using big data. Hive runs on top of Apache Hadoop and uses HDFS for storing its data. The Apache Hadoop framework is difficult to understand, and requires a different approach from traditional programming to write MapReduce-based programs. With Hive, developers do not write MapReduce at all. Hive provides an SQL-like query language called **HiveQL** to application developers, enabling them to quickly write ad-hoc queries similar to RDBMS SQL queries.

Apache Hadoop nodes communicate with each other through **Apache ZooKeeper**. It forms a mandatory part of the Apache Hadoop ecosystem. Apache ZooKeeper is responsible for maintaining co-ordination among various nodes. Besides coordinating among nodes, it also maintains configuration information and the group services to the distributed system. Apache ZooKeeper can be used independent of Hadoop, unlike other components of the ecosystem. Due to its in-memory management of information, it offers distributed co-ordination at a high speed.

Apache Mahout is an open source machine learning software library that can effectively empower Hadoop users with analytical capabilities, such as clustering and data mining, over a distributed Hadoop cluster. Mahout is highly effective over large datasets; the algorithms provided by Mahout are highly optimized to run the MapReduce framework over HDFS.

Processing Big Data Using Hadoop and MapReduce

Apache HCatalog provides metadata management services on top of Apache Hadoop. It means that all the software that runs on Hadoop can effectively use HCatalog to store the corresponding schemas in HDFS. HCatalog helps any third-party software to create, edit, and expose (using REST APIs) the generated metadata or table definitions. So, any users or scripts can run on Hadoop effectively without actually knowing where the data is physically stored on HDFS. HCatalog provides **DDL** (which stands for **Data Definition Language**) commands with which the requested MapReduce, Pig, and Hive jobs can be queued for execution, and later monitored for progress as and when required.

Apache Ambari provides a set of tools to monitor the Apache Hadoop cluster, hiding the complexities of the Hadoop framework. It offers features such as installation wizard, system alerts and metrics, provisioning and management of the Hadoop cluster, and job performances. Ambari exposes RESTful APIs to administrators to allow integration with any other software. **Apache Oozie** is a workflow scheduler used for Hadoop jobs. It can be used with MapReduce as well as Pig scripts to run the jobs. **Apache Chukwa** is another monitoring application for distributed large systems. It runs on top of HDFS and MapReduce.

Apache Sqoop is a tool designed to load large datasets into Hadoop efficiently. Apache Sqoop allows application developers to import/export easily from specific data sources, such as relational databases, enterprise data warehouses, and custom applications. Apache Sqoop internally uses a map task to perform data import/export effectively on a Hadoop cluster. Each mapper loads/unloads a slice of data across HDFS and a data source. Apache Sqoop establishes connectivity between non-Hadoop data sources and HDFS.

Apache Flume provides a framework to populate Hadoop with data from non-conventional data sources. Typical usage of Apache Fume could be for log aggregation. Apache Flume is a distributed data collection service that extracts data from the heterogeneous sources, aggregates the data, and stores it into the HDFS. Most of the time, Apache Flume is used as an **ETL** (which stands for **Extract-Transform-Load**) utility at various implementations of the Hadoop cluster.

Configuring Apache Hadoop

Setting up a Hadoop cluster is a step-by-step process. It is recommended to start with a single node setup and then extend it to the cluster mode. Apache Hadoop can be installed with three different types of setup:

- **Single node setup**: In this mode, Hadoop can be set up on a single standalone machine. This mode is used by developers for evaluation, testing, basic development, and so on.

Chapter 1

- **Pseudo distributed setup**: Apache Hadoop can be set up on a single machine with a distributed configuration. In this setup, Apache Hadoop can run with multiple Hadoop processes (daemons) on the same machine. Using this mode, developers can do the testing for a distributed setup on a single machine.
- **Fully distributed setup**: In this mode, Apache Hadoop is set up on a cluster of nodes, in a fully distributed manner. Typically, production-level setups use this mode for actively using the Hadoop computing capabilities.

> In Linux, Apache Hadoop can be set up through the root user, which makes it globally available, or as a separate user, which makes it available to only that user (Hadoop user), and the access can later be extended for other users. It is better to use a separate user with limited privileges to ensure that the Hadoop runtime does not have any impact on the running system.

Prerequisites

Before setting up a Hadoop cluster, it is important to ensure that all prerequisites are addressed. Hadoop runs on the following operating systems:

- All Linux Flavors are supported for development as well as production.
- In the case of Windows, Microsoft Windows 2008 onwards are supported. Apache Hadoop version 2.2 onwards support Windows. The older versions of Hadoop have limited support through Cygwin.

Apache Hadoop requires the following software:

- Java 1.6 onwards are all supported; however, there are compatibility issues, so it is best to look at Hadoop's Java compatibility wiki page at http://wiki.apache.org/Hadoop/HadoopJavaVersions.
- **Secure shell (ssh)** is needed to run start, stop, status, or other such scripts across a cluster. You may also consider using parallel-ssh (more information is available at https://code.google.com/p/parallel-ssh/) for connectivity.

Apache Hadoop can be downloaded from http://www.apache.org/dyn/closer.cgi/Hadoop/common/. Make sure that you download and choose the correct release from different releases, that is, one that is a stable release, the latest beta/alpha release, or a legacy stable version. You can choose to download the package or download the source, compile it on your OS, and then install it. Using operating system package installer, install the Hadoop package. This software can be installed directly by using apt-get/dpkg for Ubuntu/Debian or rpm for Red Hat/Oracle Linux from the respective sites. In the case of a cluster setup, this software should be installed on all the machines.

[9]

Setting up ssh without passphrase

Apache Hadoop uses ssh to run its scripts on different nodes, it is important to make this ssh login happen without any prompt for password. If you already have a key generated, then you can skip this step. To make ssh work without a password, run the following commands:

`$ ssh-keygen -t dsa`

You can also use RSA-based encryption algorithm (link to know about RSA: http://en.wikipedia.org/wiki/RSA_%28cryptosystem%29) instead of DSA (Digital Signature Algorithm) for your ssh authorization key creation. (For more information about differences between these two algorithms, visit http://security.stackexchange.com/questions/5096/rsa-vs-dsa-for-ssh-authentication-keys. Keep the default file for saving the key, and do not enter a passphrase. Once the key generation is successfully complete, the next step is to authorize the key by running the following command:

`$ cat ~/.ssh/id_dsa.pub >> ~/.ssh/authorized_keys`

This step will actually create an authorization key with ssh, bypassing the passphrase check as shown in the following screenshot:

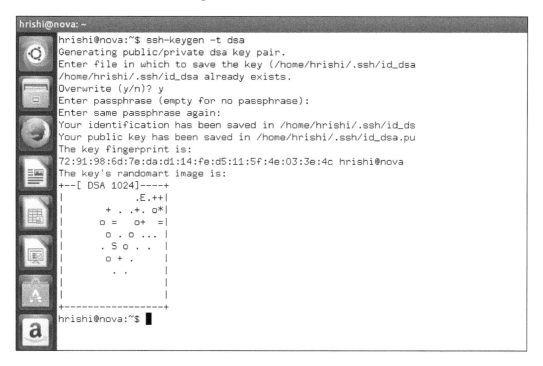

Chapter 1

Once this step is complete, you can `ssh localhost` to connect to your instance without password. If you already have a key generated, you will get a prompt to overwrite it; in such a case, you can choose to overwrite it or you can use the existing key and put it in the `authorized_keys` file.

Configuring Hadoop

Most of the Hadoop configuration is specified in the following configuration files, kept in the `$HADOOP_HOME/etc/Hadoop` folder of the installation. `$HADOOP_HOME` is the place where Apache Hadoop has been installed. If you have installed the software by using the pre-build package installer as the root user, the configuration can be found at `/etc/Hadoop`.

File Name	Description
`core-site.xml`	In this file, you can modify the default properties of Hadoop. This covers setting up different protocols for interaction, working directories, log management, security, buffers and blocks, temporary files, and so on.
`hdfs-site.xml`	This file stores the entire configuration related to HDFS. So, properties like DFS site address, data directory, replication factors, and so on are covered in these files.
`mapred-site.xml`	This file is responsible for handling the entire configuration related to the MapReduce framework. This covers the configuration for JobTracker and TaskTracker properties for Job.
`yarn-site.xml`	This file is required for managing YARN-related configuration. This configuration typically contains security/access information, proxy configuration, resource manager configuration, and so on.
`httpfs-site.xml`	Hadoop supports REST-based data transfer between clusters through an HttpFS server. This file is responsible for storing configuration related to the HttpFS server.
`fair-scheduler.xml`	This file contains information about user allocations and pooling information for the fair scheduler. It is currently under development.
`capacity-scheduler.xml`	This file is mainly used by the RM in Hadoop for setting up the scheduling parameters of job queues.
`Hadoop-env.sh` or `Hadoop-env.cmd`	All the environment variables are defined in this file; you can change any of the environments: namely the Java location, Hadoop configuration directory, and so on.
`mapred-env.sh` or `mapred-env.cmd`	This file contains the environment variables used by Hadoop while running MapReduce.

[11]

Processing Big Data Using Hadoop and MapReduce

File Name	Description
`yarn-env.sh or yarn-env.cmd`	This file contains the environment variables used by the YARN daemon that starts/stops the node manager and the RM.
`httpfs-env.sh or httpfs-env.cmd`	This file contains environment variables required by the HttpFS server.
`Hadoop-policy.xml`	This file is used to define various access control lists for Hadoop services. It controls who can use the Hadoop cluster for execution.
`Masters/slaves`	In this file, you can define the hostname for the masters and the slaves. The masters file lists all the masters, and the slaves file lists the slave nodes. To run Hadoop in the cluster mode, you need to modify these files to point to the respective master and slaves on all nodes.
`log4j.properties`	You can define various log levels for your instance; this is helpful while developing or debugging Hadoop programs. You can define levels for logging.
`common-logging.properties`	This file specifies the default logger used by Hadoop; you can override it to use your logger.

The file names marked in *pink italicized* letters will be modified while setting up your basic Hadoop cluster.

Now, let's start with the configuration of these files for the first Hadoop run. Open `core-sites.xml`, and add the following entry in it:

```
<configuration>
  <property>
    <name>fs.defaultFS</name>
    <value>hdfs://localhost:9000</value>
  </property>
</configuration>
```

This snippet tells the Hadoop framework to run inter-process communication on port 9000. Next, edit `hdfs-site.xml` and add the following entries:

```
<configuration>
  <property>
    <name>dfs.replication</name>
    <value>1</value>
  </property>
</configuration>
```

This tells HDFS to have the distributed file system's replication factor as 1. Later when you run Hadoop in the cluster configuration, you can change this replication count. The choice of replication factor varies from case to case, but if you are not sure about it, it is better to keep it as 3. This means that each document will have a replication of factor of 3.

Let's start looking at the MapReduce configuration. Some applications such as Apache HBase use only HDFS for storage, and they do not rely on the MapReduce framework. This means that all they require is the HDFS configuration, and the next configuration can be skipped.

Now, edit `mapred-site.xml` and add the following entries:

```
<configuration>
  <property>
    <name>mapreduce.framework.name</name>
    <value>yarn</value>
  </property>
</configuration>
```

This entry points to YARN as the MapReduce framework used. Further, modify `yarn-site.xml` with the following entries:

```
<configuration>
  <property>
    <name>yarn.nodemanager.aux-services</name>
    <value>mapreduce_shuffle</value>
  </property>
</configuration>
```

Processing Big Data Using Hadoop and MapReduce

This entry enables YARN to use the `ShuffleHandler` service with `nodemanager`. Once the configuration is complete, we are good to start the Hadoop. Here are the default ports used by Apache Hadoop:

Particular	Default Port
HDFS Port	9000/8020
NameNode – Web Application	50070
Data Node	50075
Secondary NameNode	50090
Resource Manager Web Application	8088

Running Hadoop

Before setting up the HDFS, we must ensure that Hadoop is configured for the pseudo-distributed mode, as per the previous section, that is, Configuring Hadoop. Set up the `JAVA_HOME` and `HADOOP_PREFIX` environment variables in your profile before you proceed. To set up a single node configuration, first you will be required to format the underlying HDFS file system; this can be done by running the following command:

```
$ $HADOOP_PREFIX/bin/hdfs namenode –format
```

Once the formatting is complete, simply try running HDFS with the following command:

```
$ $HADOOP_PREFIX/sbin/start-dfs.sh
```

The `start-dfs.sh` script file will start the name node, data node, and secondary name node on your machine through ssh. The Hadoop daemon log output is written to the `$HADOOP_LOG_DIR` folder, which by default points to `$HADOOP_HOME/logs`. Once the Hadoop daemon starts running, you will find three different processes running when you check the snapshot of the running processes. Now, browse the web interface for the NameNode; by default, it is available at `http://localhost:50070/`. You will see a web page similar to the one shown as follows with the HDFS information:

Chapter 1

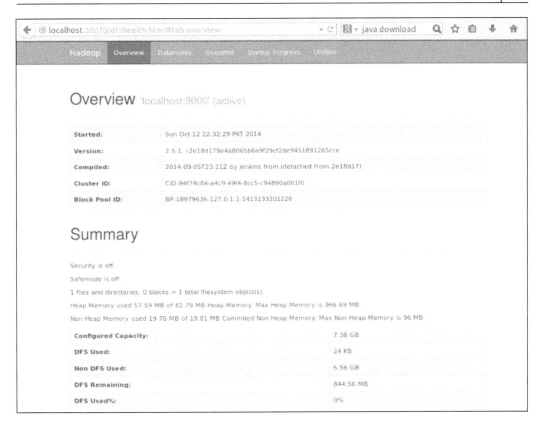

Once the HDFS is set and started, you can use all Hadoop commands to perform file system operations. The next job is to start the MapReduce framework, which includes the node manager and RM. This can be done by running the following command:

```
$ $HADOOP_PREFIX/bin/start-yarn.sh
```

Processing Big Data Using Hadoop and MapReduce

You can access the RM web page by accessing `http://localhost:8088/`. The following screenshot shows a newly set-up Hadoop RM page.

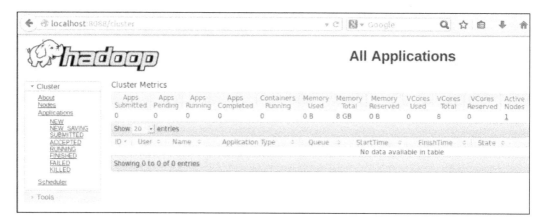

We are good to use this Hadoop setup for development now.

>
> **Safe Mode**
> When a cluster is started, NameNode starts its complete functionality only when the configured minimum percentage of blocks satisfies the minimum replication. Otherwise, it goes into safe mode. When NameNode is in the safe mode state, it does not allow any modification to its file systems. This mode can be turned off manually by running the following command:
> `$ Hadoop dfsadmin - safemode leave`

You can test the instance by running the following commands:

This command will create a test folder, so you need to ensure that this folder is not present on a server instance:

```
$ bin/Hadoop dfs -mkdir /test
```

This will create a folder. Now, load some files by using the following command:

```
$ bin/Hadoop dfs -put <file-location> test/input
```

Now, run the shipped example of wordcount that is packaged with the Hadoop deployment:

```
$ bin/Hadoop jar share/Hadoop/mapreduce/Hadoop-mapreduce-examples-2.5.1.jar test/input test/output
```

Chapter 1

A successful run will create the output in HDFS's test/output/part-r-00000 file. You can view the output by downloading this file from HDFS to a local machine.

Setting up a Hadoop cluster

In this case, assuming that you already have a single node setup as explained in the previous sections, with ssh being enabled, you just need to change all the slave configurations to point to the master. This can be achieved by first introducing the slaves file in the $HADOOP_PREFIX/etc/Hadoop folder. Similarly, on all slaves, you require the master file in the $HADOOP_PREFIX/etc/Hadoop folder to point to your master server hostname.

> While adding new entries for the hostname, one must ensure that the firewall is disabled to allow remote nodes access to different ports. Alternatively, specific ports can be opened/modified by modifying the Hadoop configuration files. Similarly, all the names of nodes that are participating in the cluster should be resolvable through **DNS** (which stands for **Domain Name System**), or through the /etc/host entries of Linux.

Once this is ready, let us change the configuration files. Open core-sites.xml, and add the following entry in it:

```
<configuration>
  <property>
    <name>fs.defaultFS</name>
    <value>hdfs://master-server:9000</value>
  </property>
</configuration>
```

All other configuration is optional. Now, run the servers in the following order: First, you need to format your storage for the cluster; use the following command to do so:

$ $HADOOP_PREFIX/bin/Hadoop dfs namenode -format <Name of Cluster>

This formats the name node for a new cluster. Once the name node is formatted, the next step is to ensure that DFS is up and connected to each node. Start namenode, followed by the data nodes:

$ $HADOOP_PREFIX/sbin/Hadoop-daemon.sh start namenode

Similarly, the datanode can be started from all the slaves.

$ $HADOOP_PREFIX/sbin/Hadoop-daemon.sh start datanode

Keep track of the log files in the $HADOOP_PREFIX/logs folder in order to see that there are no exceptions. Once the HDFS is available, namenode can be accessed through the web as shown here:

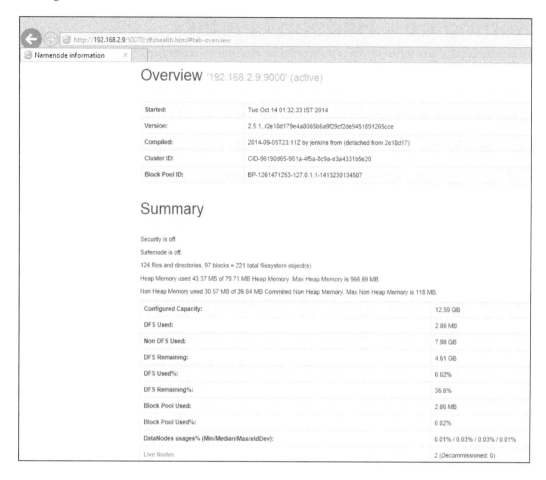

The next step is to start YARN and its associated applications. First, start with the RM:

`$ $HADOOP_YARN_HOME/sbin/yarn-daemon.sh start resourcemanager`

Each node must run an instance of one node manager. To run the node manager, use the following command:

`$ $HADOOP_YARN_HOME/sbin/yarn-daemon.sh start nodemanager`

Optionally, you can also run Job History Server on the Hadoop cluster by using the following command:

`$ $HADOOP_PREFIX/sbin/mr-jobhistory-daemon.sh start historyserver`

Once all instances are up, you can see the status of the cluster on the web through the RM UI as shown in the following screenshot. The complete setup can be tested by running the simple wordcount example.

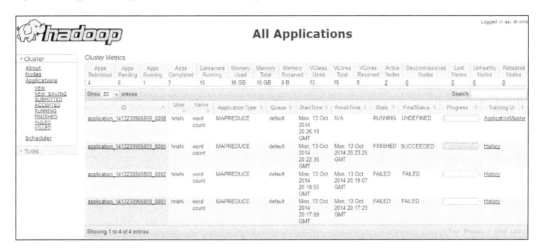

This way, your cluster is set up and is ready to run with multiple nodes. For advanced setup instructions, do visit the Apache Hadoop website at http://Hadoop.apache.org.

Common problems and their solutions

The following is a list of common problems and their solutions:

- **When I try to format the HDFS node, I get the exception java.io.IOException: Incompatible clusterIDs in namenode and datanode?**

    This issue usually appears if you have a different/older cluster and you are trying to format a new namenode; however, the datanodes still point to older cluster ids. This can be handled by one of the following:

    1. By deleting the DFS data folder, you can find the location from hdfs-site.xml and restart the cluster
    2. By modifying the version file of HDFS usually located at <HDFS-STORAGE-PATH>/hdfs/datanode/current/
    3. By formatting namenode with the problematic datanode's cluster ID:

        ```
        $ hdfs namenode -format -clusterId <cluster-id>
        ```

- **My Hadoop instance is not starting up with the ./start-all.sh script? When I try to access the web application, it shows the page not found error?**

  This could be happening because of a number of issues. To understand the issue, you must look at the Hadoop logs first. Typically, Hadoop logs can be accessed from the `/var/log` folder if the precompiled binaries are installed as the root user. Otherwise, they are available inside the Hadoop installation folder.

- **I have setup N node clusters, and I am running the Hadoop cluster with ./start-all.sh. I am not seeing many nodes in the YARN/NameNode web application?**

  This again can be happening due to multiple reasons. You need to verify the following:

  1. Can you reach (connect to) each of the cluster nodes from namenode by using the IP address/machine name? If not, you need to have an entry in the `/etc/hosts` file.
  2. Is the ssh login working without password? If not, you need to put the authorization keys in place to ensure logins without password.
  3. Is datanode/nodemanager running on each of the nodes, and can you connect to namenode/AM? You can validate this by running ssh on the node running namenode/AM.
  4. If all these are working fine, you need to check the logs and see if there are any exceptions as explained in the previous question.
  5. Based on the log errors/exceptions, specific action has to be taken.

Summary

In this chapter, we discussed the need for Apache Hadoop to address the challenging problems faced by today's world. We looked at Apache Hadoop and its ecosystem, and we focused on how to configure Apache Hadoop, followed by running it. Finally, we created Hadoop clusters by using a simple set of instructions. The next chapter is all about Apache Solr, which has brought a revolution in the search and analytics domain.

Understanding Apache Solr

In the previous chapter, we discussed how big data has evolved to cater to the needs of various organizations, in order to deal with a humongous data size. There are many other challenges while working with data of different shapes. For example, the log files of any application server have semi-structured data or Microsoft Word documents, making it difficult to store the data in traditional relational storage. The challenge to handling such data is not just related to storage: there is also the big question of how to access the required information. Enterprise search engines are designed to address this problem.

Today, finding the required information within a specified timeframe has become more crucial than ever. Enterprises without information retrieval capabilities suffer from problems such as lost productivity of employees, poor decisions based on faulty/incomplete information, duplicated efforts, and so on. Given these scenarios, it is evident that Enterprise searches are absolutely necessary in any enterprise.

Apache Solr is an open source enterprise search platform, designed to handle these problems in an efficient and scalable way. Apache Solr is built on top of Apache Lucene, which provides an open source information search and retrieval library. Today, many professional enterprise search market leaders, such as LucidWorks and PolySpot, have built their search platform using Apache Solr. We will be learning more about Apache Solr in this chapter, and we will be looking at the following aspects of Apache Solr:

- Setting up Apache Solr
- Apache Solr architecture
- Configuring Solr
- Loading data in Apache Solr
- Querying for information in Solr

Setting up Apache Solr

We will be going through the Apache Solr architecture in the next section; for now, let's install Apache Solr on our machines. Apache Solr is a Java Servlet web application that runs on Apache Lucene, Tika, and other open source libraries. Apache Solr ships with a demo server on jetty, so one can simply run it through the command line. This helps users to run the Solr instance quickly. However, you can choose to customize it and deploy it in your own environment. Apache Solr does not ship with any installer; it has to be run as a part of J2EE Application.

Prerequisites for setting up Apache Solr

Apache Solr requires Java 1.6 or more to run, so it is important to make sure you have the correct version of Java by calling `java -version`, as shown in the following screenshot:

```
hrishi@nova:~$ java -version
java version "1.6.0_32"
OpenJDK Runtime Environment (IcedTea6 1.13.4) (6b32-1.13.4-4ubuntu0.14.04.1)
OpenJDK Client VM (build 23.25-b01, mixed mode, sharing)
hrishi@nova:~$
```

> With the latest version of Apache Solr (4.0 or more), JDK 1.5 is not supported anymore. Apache Solr 4.0+ runs on JDK 1.6 + version. Instead of going for the pre-shipped JDK with your default operating system, go for the full version of JDK by downloading it from http://www.oracle.com/technetwork/java/javase/downloads/index.html?ssSourceSiteId=otnjp. This will enable full support for an international charset. Apache Solr 4.10.1 version requires a minimum of JDK 7.

Once you have the correct Java version, you need a servlet container such as Tomcat, Jetty, Resin, Glassfish, or Weblogic installed on your machine. If you intend to use a jetty-based demo server, then you would not require a container.

Running Apache Solr on jetty

The Apache Solr distribution comes as a single zipped folder. You can download the stable installer from `http://lucene.apache.org/solr/` or from its nightly builds running on the same site. To run Solr in Windows, download the zip file from the Apache mirror site for Linux, UNIX, and other such flavors; you can download the `.gzip/.tgz` version. In Windows, you can simply unzip your file, and in UNIX, you can run the following command:

```
$ tar -xvzf solr-<major-minor version>.tgz
```

Another way is to build Apache Solr from a source. This will be required if you are going to modify or extend the Apache Solr source for your own handler, plugin, and others. You need Java SE 7 JDK (which stands for Java Development Kit) or JRE (which stands for Java Runtime Environment), Apache Ant distribution (1.8.2 or more), and Apache Ivy (2.2.0+). You can compile the source by simply navigating to the Solr folder and running ant from there.

> More information can be found at `https://wiki.apache.org/solr/HowToCompileSolr`

When you unzip Solr, it extracts the following folders:

- `contrib/`: This folder contains all the libraries that are additional to Solr, and they can be included on demand. They provide libraries for data import handler, MapReduce, Apache UIMA, velocity template, and so on.
- `dist/`: This folder provides the distributions of Solr and other useful libraries such as SolrJ, UIMA, and MapReduce. We will be looking at this in the next chapter.
- `docs/`: This folder contains documentation for Apache Solr.
- `example/`: This folder provides jetty-based Solr web apps that can be directly used. We are going to use this folder for running Apache Solr.
- `licenses/`: This folder contains all the licenses of the underlying libraries used by Solr.

Now, declare `$JAVA_HOME` to point to your JDK/JRE. You will find the jetty server in the `solr<version>/example` folder. Once you unzip `solr-<major-minor version>.tgz`, all you need to do is go to `solr<version>/example` and run the following command:

```
$ $JAVA_HOME/bin/java -jar start.jar
```

Understanding Apache Solr

>
> If you are using the latest release of Solr (Solr 5.0), you need to go to the `solr-5.0.0` folder and run the following command:
>
> **$ bin/slor start**
>
> The instructions for Solr 5.0 are available at:
>
> https://cwiki.apache.org/confluence/display/solr/Solr+Start+Script+Reference

The default jetty instance will run on port 8983, and you can access the Solr instance by visiting the following URL: `http://localhost:8983/Solr/browse`. It shows a default search screen as shown in the following screenshot:

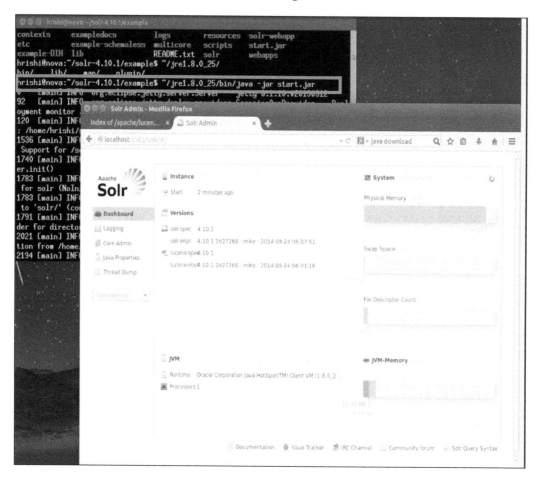

If your system default is Locale, or character set is non-English (that is, en/en-US), for the sake of safety you can override your system defaults for Solr by passing -`Duser.language=en` -`Duser.country=US` in your jetty to ensure smooth running of Solr.

Running Solr on other J2EE containers

It is relatively easy to set up Apache Solr on any J2EE container. It requires deployment of the Apache Solr application war file using the standard J2EE application deployment of any container. Another additional step that the Apache Solr application needs is the location of the Apache Solr home folder. This can either be set through Java options by setting the following environment variables or updating the container start up script:

```
$ export JAVA_OPTS="$JAVA_OPTS -Dsolr.solr.home=/opt/solr/example"
```

Alternatively, you can configure JNDI lookup for the `java:comp/env/solr/home` resource by pointing it to the Solr home folder. In Tomcat, this can be done by creating a context XML file with a chosen name (`context.xml`) in `$CATALINA_HOME/conf/Catalina/localhost/context.xml`, and adding the following entries:

```
<?xml version="1.0" encoding="utf-8"?>
<Context docBase="<solr-home>/example/solr/solr.war" debug="0"
crossContext="true">
  <Environment name="solr/home" type="java.lang.String" value="<solr-
home>/example/solr" override="true"/>
</Context>
```

Hello World with Apache Solr!

Once you are done with the installation of Apache Solr, you can simply run examples by going to the `examples/exampledocs` folder and running:

```
java -jar post.jar solr.xml monitor.xml
```

Understanding Apache Solr

`post.jar` is a utility provided by Solr to upload the data to Apache Solr for indexing. When it is run, the `post.jar` file simply uploads all the files that are passed as a parameter to Apache Solr for indexing, and Solr indexes these files and stores them in its repository. Now, try accessing your instance by typing `http://localhost:8983/solr/browse`; you should find a sample search interface with some information in it, as shown in the following screenshot:

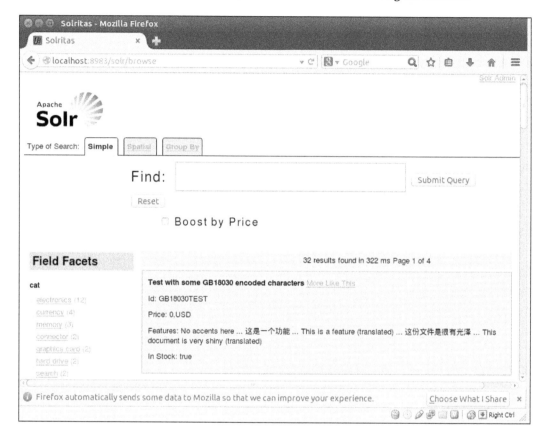

Chapter 2

Understanding Solr administration

Apache Solr provides an excellent user interface for administrating the server and can be accessed by calling `http://localhost:8983/solr`. Apache Solr has the concepts of Collections and Core. A **collection** in Apache Solr is a collection of Solr documents that represent one complete logical index. Solr **Core** is an execution unit of Solr that can run on its own configuration and other metadata. Apache Solr collections can be created for each index. Similarly, you can run Solr in multiple core modes.

Option	Purpose
Dashboard	This shows information related to version, memory consumption, JVM, and so on.
Logging	Shows log outputs with the latest logs on top
Logging | Level	Shows the current log configuration for packages, that is, for which packages the logs are enabled
Core Admin	Shows information about core, and allows its administration
Java Properties	Shows different Java properties set when Solr is running
Thread Dump	Describes the stack trace with information on CPU and user time; also enables a detailed stack trace
collection1	Demonstrates different parameters of collection, and all the activities you can perform, such as running queries and ping status

Solr navigation

The following table shows some of the important URLs configured with Apache Solr by default:

URL	Purpose
/select	For processing search queries, the primary request handler provided with Solr is "SearchHandler." It delegates to a sequence of search components.
/query	Same SearchHandler for JSON-based requests.
/get	Real-time get handler, guaranteed to return the latest stored fields of any document, without the need to commit or open a new searcher. The current implementation relies on the updateLog feature being enabled in the JSON format.
/browse	This URL provides a faceted web-based search, primary interface.
/update/extract	Solr accepts posted XML messages that Add/Replace, Commit, Delete, and Delete by query, by using the /update URL (ExtractingRequestHandler).
/update/csv	This URL is specific for CSV messages, CSVRequestHandler.

[27]

Understanding Apache Solr

URL	Purpose
/update/json	This URL is specific for messages in the JSON format, JsonUpdateRequestHandler.
/analysis/field	This URL provides an interface for analyzing the fields. It provides the ability to specify multiple field types and field names in the same request, and outputs index-time and query-time analysis for each of them. It also uses FieldAnalysisRequestHandler internally.
/analysis/document	This URL provides an interface for analyzing the documents.
/admin	AdminHandler for providing the administration of Solr. AdminHandler has multiple sub-handlers defined. /admin/ping is for the health checkup.
/debug/dump	DumpRequestHandler — Echoes the request content back to the client.
/replication	Supports replicating indexes across different Solr servers, used by masters and slaves for data sharing. Uses ReplicationHandler.

Common problems and solutions

In this section, we will try and understand the common problems faced while running Solr instances:

- **When we run Apache Solr, I get the following error:**

  ```
  Java.lang.UnsupportedClassError: org.apache.solr.servlet.
  SolrDispatchFilter : Org.eclipse.jetty.Unsupported Major-Minor
  version 51
  ```

  This error is seen due to a Java version mismatch with an Apache Solr-compiled Java version. In this case, you need Java Version 7 or more. The following values are the Java versions with class version mapping:

  ```
  J2SE 8 = 52,
  J2SE 7 = 51,
  J2SE 6.0 = 50,
  J2SE 5.0 = 49,
  JDK 1.4 = 48,
  JDK 1.3 = 47,
  JDK 1.2 = 46,
  JDK 1.1 = 45
  ```

So, you need to use Java Version 7 to run Apache Solr. If you have any other Java run-time setup on your machine for the existing applications, and do not wish to disturb it, simply download JRE in a folder and run the Solr start command (as explained in the previous section) by calling Java of the new JRE.

- While running Solr, I got `java.lang.OutOfMemoryError`. How to fix it?

  The Out-of-Memory error is thrown by the Java Virtual Machine (JVM) running Apache Solr when there is not enough memory available for heap, or for PermGen (Permanent Generation Space holds metadata regarding user classes and methods). When you get such an error, you need to restart the container. However, while restarting the container, you must make sure that you increase the memory of JVM. This can be done by adding the following JVM arguments for PermGen:

  ```
  export JVM_ARGS="-Xmx1024m -XX:MaxPermSize=256m"
  ```

  For correcting the heap space error, you can specify the following JVM arguments:

  ```
  export JVM_ARGS="-Xms1024m -Xmx1024m"
  ```

  Please note that the size of memory should be specified by the user. Visit `http://jvmmemory.com/` to create these JVM arguments for setting the correct JVM variables.

The Apache Solr architecture

An Apache Solr instance can run as a single core or multicore; it is a client server model. A Solr core is nothing but the running instance of a Solr index along with its configuration. Earlier, Apache Solr had a single core that in turn limited the consumers to run Solr on one application, through a single schema and configuration file. Later, support for creating multiple cores was added. With this support one can now run one Solr instance for multiple schemas and configurations with unified administrations. You can run Solr in multicore with the following command:

```
java -Dsolr.solr.home=multicore -jar start.jar
```

Understanding Apache Solr

Apache Solr is composed of multiple modules, some of them being separate projects in themselves. Let's understand the different components of the Apache Solr architecture. The following diagram depicts the Apache Solr conceptual architecture:

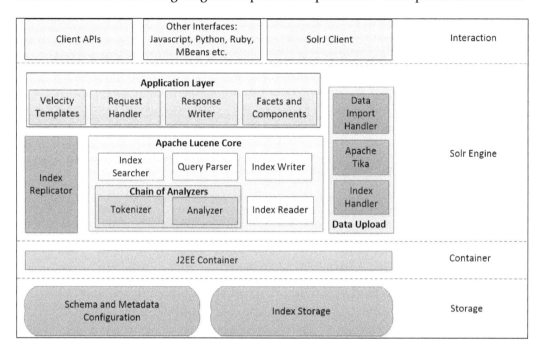

Apache Solr can run in a master-slave mode. **Index replicator** is responsible for distributing indexes across multiple slaves. The master server maintains index updating, and slaves are responsible for talking with the master to get them replicated for high availability. **Apache Lucene core** gets packages as a library with the Apache Solr application. It provides the core functionalities for Solr, such as index, query processing, searching data, ranking matched results, and returning them.

Apache Lucene comes with a variety of query implementations. **Query Parser** is responsible for parsing the queries passed by the end search as the search string. Lucene provides TermQuery, BooleanQuery, PhraseQuery, PrefixQuery, RangeQuery, MultiTermQuery, FilteredQuery, SpanQuery, and so on as query implementations.

Index Searcher is a basic component of Solr searched with a default base searcher class. This class is responsible for returning ordered matched results of the searched keyword ranked, as per the computed score. **Index Reader** provides access to indexes stored in the file system. It can be used for searching for an index. Similar to Index Searcher, **Index Writer** allows you to create and maintain indexes in Apache Lucene.

Analyzer is responsible for examining the fields and generating tokens. **Tokenizer** breaks field data into lexical units or tokens. **Filter** examines a field of tokens from Tokenizer and either keeps them, transforms them, discards them, or creates new ones. Tokenizers and Filters together form a **chain** or **pipeline of Analyzers**. There can only be one Tokenizer per Analyzer. The output of one chain is fed to another. The Analyzer process is used for indexing as well as querying by Solr. They play an important role in speeding up the query as well as index time and finding the right set of matches; they also reduce the amount of data that gets generated out of these operations. You can define your own customer as Analyzers depending upon your use case.

Query Parser is responsible for parsing the queries and converting them into Lucene Query Objects. There are different types of parsers available, such as lucene, DisMax, and edismax. Each parser offers different functionalities and can be used on the basis of particular requirements. Once a query is parsed, it hands it over to index **searcher**. The job of index reader is to run the queries on index store, gather the results, and send them to response writer. **Response Writer** is responsible for responding to the client; it formats the query response on the basis of search outcomes from the Lucene engine.

Index Handler is a type of update handler, handling the tasks of add, update, and delete documents for indexing. Apache Solr supports updates through index handler in the JSON, XML, and plaintext formats.

Data Import Handler (**DIH**) provides a mechanism for integrating different data sources with Apache Solr for indexing. The data sources could be relational databases or web-based sources (for example, RSS, ATOM feeds, and e-mails).

Although DIH is a part of Solr development, the default installation does not include it in the Solr application; it needs to be included in the application explicitly. We will be looking at **Apache Tika** in detail in the following sections.

Configuring Solr

Apache Solr allows extensive configuration to meet the needs of the consumer. Configuring the instance revolves around the following:

- Defining a schema
- Configuring Solr parameters

First, let's try and understand the Apache Solr structure, and then, look at all these steps to understand the configuration of Apache Solr.

Understanding the Solr structure

The Apache Solr home folder mainly contains the configuration and index-related data. These are the following major folders in the Solr collection:

Directory	Purpose
`conf/`	This folder contains all the configuration files of Apache Solr and is mandatory. Among them, `solrconfig.xml`, and `schema.xml` are important configuration files.
`data/`	This folder stores the data related to indexes generated by Solr. This is a default location for Solr to store this information. This location can be overridden by modifying `conf/solrconfig.xml`.
`lib/`	This folder is optional. If it exists, Solr will load any Jars found in this folder and use them to resolve any "plugins" if provided in `solrconfig.xml` (Analyzers, RequestHandlers, and so on.) Alternatively, you can use the `<lib>` syntax in `conf/solrconfig.xml` to direct Solr to your plugins.

Defining the Solr schema

In an enterprise, the data is generated from all the software systems that participate in day-to-day operations. This data has different formats, and bringing in this data for big-data processing requires a storage system that is flexible enough to accommodate the data with varying data models. Traditional relational databases allow users to define a strict data structure and an SQL-based querying mechanism.

By design, Solr supports any data to be loaded in a search engine through different handlers, making it a data format agnostic. Solr can easily be scaled on top of commodity hardware; hence, it becomes one of the most efficient eligible NoSQL-based search programs available today. The data can be stored in Solr indexes and can be queried through Lucene search APIs. Solr does perform joins because of its denormalization of data. The overall schema file (`schema.xml`) is structured in the following manner:

```
<schema>
  <types>
  <fields>
  <uniqueKey>
  <defaultSearchField>
  <solrQueryParser defaultOperator>
  <copyField>
</schema>
```

Solr fields

Apache Solr's basic unit of information is a **document**, which is a set of data that describes something. Each document in Solr is composed of **Fields**. Apache Solr allows you to define the structure of your data to extend support for searching across the traditional keyword searching. You can allow Solr to understand the structure of your data (coming from various sources) by defining fields in the schema definition file. These fields, once defined, will be made available at the time of data import or data upload. The schema is stored in the schema.xml file in the conf/ folder of Apache Solr.

Apache Solr ships with a default schema.xml file, which you have to change to fit your needs.

 If you change schema.xml in a Solr instance running on some data, the impact of this change requires regeneration of the Solr index with the new schema.

In the schema configuration, you can define field types (for example, string, integer, and date) and map them to their respective Java classes:

```
<field name="id" type="integer" indexed="true" stored="true"
required="true"/>
```

This enables users to define the custom type, should they wish to. Then, you can define the fields with the name and type pointing to one of the defined types. A field in Solr will have the following major attributes:

Name	Description
Default	This sets default value, if not read while importing a document.
Indexed	This is true, when it has to be indexed (that is, can be searched and sorted, and have facets created).
Stored	When true, a field is stored in the index store, and it will be accessible while displaying results.
compressed	When true, the field will be zipped (using gzip). This is applicable for text-based fields.
multiValued	If a field contains multiple values in the same import cycle of the document/row.

Understanding Apache Solr

Name	Description
omitNorms	When true, it omits the norms associated with a field (such as length normalization, and index boosting). Similarly, it has omitTermFreqAndPositions (if true, omits term frequency, positions, and payloads from postings for this field. This can be a performance boost for fields that don't require this information. It also reduces the storage space required for the index) and omitPositions.
termVectors	When true, it stores metadata related to a document and returns this metadata when queried.

With Solr 4.2, the team has introduced a new feature called **DocValue** for fields. DocValues are a way of building an index that is more efficient for purposes like sorting and faceting. While Apache Solr relies on an inverted index mechanism, the DocValue storage focuses on efficiently indexing the document, in order to index the storage mechanism by using a column-oriented field structure, using a document-to-value mapping built at index time. This approach (column-oriented field) results in a reduction of memory usage and the overall search speed. DocValue can be enabled on specific fields in Solr in the following fashion:

```
<field name="test_outcome" type="string" indexed="false"
stored="false" docValues="true" />
```

If the data is indexed before applying DocValue, it has to be re-indexed to utilize the gains of DocValue indexing.

Dynamic fields in Solr

In addition to static fields, you can also use Solr dynamic fields for getting flexibility, in case you do not know the schema upfront. Use the `<dynamicField>` declaration for creating a field rule to allow Solr to understand which datatype is to be used. In the following sample, any field imported, and suffixed with *_no (For example, id_no and vehicle_no) will in turn be read as an integer by Solr. In this case, * represents a wildcard.

The following code snippet shows how you can create a dynamic field:

```
<dynamicField name="*_no" type="integer" indexed="true"
stored="true"/>
```

> Although it is not a mandatory condition, it is recommended for each Solr instance to have a unique identifier field for the data. Similarly, the ID name-specified unique key cannot be multivalued.

Copying the fields

You can also index the same data into multiple fields by using the <copyField> directive. This is typically needed when you want to have multi-indexing for the same data type. For example, if you have data for a refrigerator with the company name followed by the model number (WHIRLPOOL-1000LTR, SAMSUNG-980LTR, and others), you can have these indexed separately by applying your own Tokenizers to different fields. You might generate indexes for two different fields: namely Company Name and Model Number. You can define Tokenizers specific to your field types. Here is the sample `copyField` from `schema.xml`:

```
<copyField source="cat" dest="text"/>
<copyField source="name" dest="text"/>
<copyField source="manu" dest="text"/>
<copyField source="features" dest="text"/>
```

Dealing with field types

You can define your own field types in Apache Solr that cater to your requirements for data processing. The field type includes four types of information:

- Name
- Implementation class name (implemented on `org.apache.solr.schema.FieldType`)
- If the field type is TextField, a description of the field analysis for the field type
- Field attributes

The following XML snippet shows a sample field type:

```
<fieldType name="text_ws" class="solr.TextField"
  positionIncrementGap="100">
  <analyzer>
    <tokenizer class="solr.WhitespaceTokenizerFactory"/>
  </analyzer>
</fieldType>
```

[35]

Understanding Apache Solr

The class attribute indicates which Java class the given field type is associated with. `PositionIncrementGap` determines the spacing between two words. It's useful for multivalued fields where the space between multiple values of the fields is determined. For example, if the author field has "John Doe" and "Jack Williams" as values, when PositionIncrementGap is zero, a search for Doe Jack will match with these fields because Solr treats this field as John Doe Jack Williams. To separate these multivalued fields, you can specify a high PositionIncrementGap value. The name attribute indicates the name of the field type; later when a field is defined, it uses the type attribute to denote the associated field type as shown in following code snippet:

```
<field name="name" type="text_ws" indexed="true" stored="true"/>
```

Additional metadata configuration

There are other files where metadata can be specified. These files again appear in the `conf` folder of Apache Solr. These files are given in the following table:

File Name	Description
Protwords.txt	In this file, you can specify protected words that you do not wish to get stemmed. So, for example, a stemmer might stem the word catfish to cat or fish.
Currency.txt	Stores current mapping of exchange rates between different countries; this is helpful when you have your application accessed by people from different countries.
Elevate.txt	With this file, you can influence the search results and get your own results to rank among the top-ranked results. This overrides Lucene's standard ranking scheme, taking into account elevations from this file.
Spellings.txt	In this file, you can provide spelling suggestions to the end user.
Synonyms.txt	Using this file, you can specify your own synonyms. For example, `cost => money, money => dollars`.
Stopwords.txt	Stopwords are those that will not be indexed and used by Solr in the applications; this is particularly helpful when you really wish to get rid of certain words; for example: In the string "Jamie and Joseph," the word "and" can be marked as a stopword.

[36]

Chapter 2

Other important elements of the Solr schema

The following table describes the different elements in `schema.xml`:

Name	Description	Example
Unique key	The `uniqueKey` element specifies which field is a unique identifier for documents. For example, `uniqueKey` should be used if you ever update a document in the index.	`<uniqueKey>id</uniqueKey>`
Default search field	If you are using the Lucene query parser, queries that don't specify a field name will use the `defaultSearchField`. The use of default search has decreased from Apache Solr 3.6 or higher.	`<defaultSearchField></defaultSearchField>`
Similarity	Similarity is a Lucene class responsible for scoring the matched results. Solr allows you to override the default similarity behavior through the `<similarity>` declaration. Similarity can be configured at the global level; however, Solr 4.0 extends similarity to be configured at the field level.	`<similarity class="solr.DFRSimilarityFactory">` `<str name="basicModel">P</str>` `<str name="afterEffect">L</str>` `<str name="normalization">H2</str>` `<float name="c">7</float>` `</similarity>`

Configuration files of Apache Solr

The storage of Apache Solr is mainly used for storing metadata and the actual index information. It is typically a file stored locally, configured in the configuration of Apache Solr. The default Solr installation package comes with a Jetty server, whose configuration can be found in the `solr.home/conf` folder of Solr install. There are three major configuration files in Solr:

File name	Description
`Solrconfig.xml`	This is the main configuration file of your Solr install. Using this, you can control everything possible, right from caching and specifying customer handlers to codes and commit options.

[37]

Understanding Apache Solr

File name	Description
Schema.xml	This file is responsible for defining a Solr schema for your application. For example: Solr implementation for log management would have a schema with Log-related attributes, that is, log levels, severity, message type, container name, application name, and so on.
Solr.xml	Using Solr.xml, you can configure Solr cores (single or multiple) for your setup. It also provides additional parameters such as ZooKeeper timeout and transient cache size.

Apache Solr (underlying Lucene) indexing is a specially designed data structure, stored in the file system as a set of index files. The index is designed with a specific format in such a way as to maximize the query performance.

Once the schema is configured, the immediate next step is to configure the instance itself to work with your enterprise. There are two major configurations that comprise the Solr configuration, namely solrconfig.xml and solr.xml. Let's look at them one by one.

Working with solr.xml and Solr core

The solr.xml configuration resides in the $SOLR_HOME folder and mainly focuses on maintaining the configuration for logging, cloud setup, and Solr core. The Apache Solr 4.X code line uses solr.xml for identifying the cores defined by the users. In the newer versions of Solr 5.x (planned), the current solr.xml structure (which contains the <core> element and so on) will not be supported, and there will be an alternative structure used by Solr.

Instance configuration with solrconfig.xml

The solrconfig.xml file primarily provides you access to request handlers, listeners, and request dispatchers. Let's look at the solrconfig.xml file and understand all the important declarations you'd be using frequently:

Directive	Description
luceneMatchVersion	Tells which version of Lucene/Solr this configuration file is set to. When upgrading your Solr instances, you need to modify this attribute.

[38]

Directive	Description

Lib	In case you create any plugins for Solr, you need to put a library reference here, so that it gets picked up. The libraries are loaded in the same sequence as that of the configuration order. The paths are relative; you can also specify regular expressions. For example:
	
	`<lib dir=".../../../contrib/velocity/lib"`
	`regex=".*\.jar" />.`

dataDir	By default, Solr uses the `./data` folder for storing indexes; however, this can be overridden by changing the folder for data by using this directive.
indexConfig	This directive is of the complex type, and it allows you to change the settings of some of the internal indexing configuration of Solr.
Filter	You can specify different filters to be run at the time of index creation.
writeLockTimeout	This directive denotes the maximum time to wait for the write lock for IndexWriter.
maxIndexingThreads	Denotes the maximum number of indexes and threads that can run in the IndexWriter; if more threads arrive, they have to wait. The default value is 8.
ramBufferSizeMB	The maximum RAM you need in the buffer while index creation, before the files are flushed to filesystem.
maxBufferedDocs	Limits the number of documents buffered.
lockType	When indexes are generated and stored in the file, this mechanism decides which file-locking mechanism should be used to manage concurrent read-writes. There are three types of file locking mechanisms: single (one process at a time), native (native operating system driven), and simple (based on locking using plain files).
unlockOnStartup	When true, it will release all the write locks held in past.
Jmx	Solr can expose runtime statistics through MBeans. It can be enabled or disabled through this directive.
updateHandler	Update handler is responsible for managing the updates to Solr. The entire configuration for updateHandler forms a part of this directive.
updateLog	You can specify the folder and other configuration for transaction logs while the index updates.

Understanding Apache Solr

Directive	Description
autoCommit	Enables automatic commit, when updates are happening. This could be based on documents or time before an automatic commit is triggered.
Listener	Using this directive, you can subscribe to update events when IndexWriters are updating the index. The listeners can either be run at the time of "postCommit" or "postOptimize"
Query	This directive is mainly responsible for controlling different parameters at the query time.
requestDispatcher	By setting parameters in this directive, you can control how a request will be processed by SolrDispatchFilter.
requestHandler	Request handlers are responsible for handling different types of requests with a specific logic for Apache Solr. These are described in a separate section.
searchComponent	Search components in Solr enable additional logic that can be used by the search handler to provide a better searching experience. These are described in *Appendix, Use Cases for Big Data Search*.
updateRequestProcessorChain	Update request processor chain defines how update requests are processed; you can define your own updateRequestProcessor to perform tasks such as cleaning up data and optimizing text fields.
queryResponseWriter	Each request for query is formatted and written back to the user through queryResponseWriter. You can extend your Solr instance to have responses for XML, JSON, PHP, Ruby, Python, csvs, and so on by enabling the respective pre-defined writers. If you have a custom requirement for a certain type of response, it can easily be extended.
queryParser	The query parser directive tells Apache Solr which query parser to be used for parsing the query and creating Lucene Query Objects. Apache Solr contains pre-defined query parsers such as lucene (default), DisMax (based on weights of fields), edismax (similar to DisMax with some additional features), and others.

Understanding the Solr plugin

Apache Solr provides easy extensions to its current architecture through Solr plugins. Using Solr plugins, one can load his or her own code to perform a variety of tasks within Solr: from custom Request Handlers to process searches, to custom Analyzers and Token Filters for the text field. Typically, the plugins can be developed in Solr by using any IDE by importing apache-solr*.jar as the library.

The following types of plugins can be created with Apache Solr:

Component	Description
Search components	These plugins operate on a result set of a query. The results that they produce typically appear at the end of the search request.
Request handler	Request handlers are used to provide a REST endpoint from the Solr instance to get some work done.
Filters	Filters are the chain of agents that analyze the text for various filtering criteria, such as lower case and stemming. Now you can introduce your own filter and package it along with the plugin jar file.

Once the plugin is developed, it has to be defined as a part of solrconfig.xml by pointing the library to your jar.

Other configuration

Request handlers in Solr are responsible for handling requests. Each request handler can be associated with one relative URL: for example, /search, /select. A request handler that provides search capabilities is called a search handler. There are more than 25 request handlers available with Solr by default, and you can see the complete list here: http://lucene.apache.org/solr/api/org/apache/solr/request/SolrRequestHandler.html.

There are search handlers that provide searching capabilities on a Solr-based index (For example, DisMaxRequestHandler and SearchHandler); similarly, there are update handlers that provide support for uploading documents to Solr (For example, DataImportHandler and CSVUpdateRequestHandler). RealTimeGetHandler provides the latest stored fields of any document. UpdateRequestHandlers are responsible to process the updating of an index. Similarly, CSVRequestHandler and JsonUpdateRequestHandler take the responsibility of updating the indexes with the CSV and JSON formats. ExtractingRequestHandler uses Apache Tika to extract the text from different file formats.

Understanding Apache Solr

Loading data in Apache Solr

Once Apache Solr is configured, the next step is to load data in Apache Solr and run queries. There are different ways to load data into Apache Solr. The following diagram depicts most of the used ones:

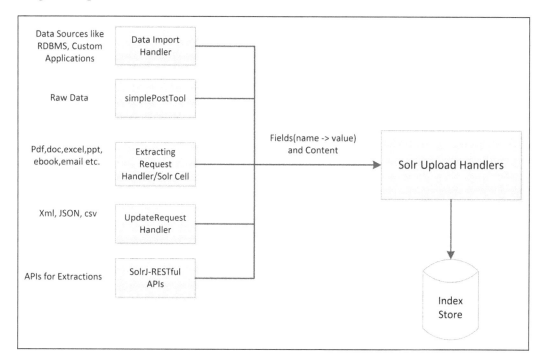

We have already seen the simple post tool earlier while setting up Apache Solr. We are going to understand Extracting Request Handler.

Extracting request handler – Solr Cell

Solr Cell is one of the most powerful handlers for uploading any type of data. This is particularly useful if you wish to run Solr on a set of files/unstructured data containing different formats such as office, pdf, eBook, emails, and text. In Apache Tika, text extraction is based purely on file type and content. So, if you have a PDF of scanned images containing text, Apache Tika won't be able to extract any of the text from it. In such cases, you need to use OCR-based software to bring in such functionality for Solr. You can simply try this by downloading the curl utility and then by running it on your document.

```
curl 'http://localhost:8983/solr/update/extract?literal.
id=doc1&commit=true' -F "myfile=@<your document name with extension>"
```

Index handlers such as Simple Post Tool, Update Request Handler, and SolrJ provide the add, update, and delete of documents to the index for the XML, JSON, and CSV formats. Update Request Handler provides a web-based URL for uploading the document. This can be done through the curl utility.

 `curl/wget` utilities can be used for uploading data to Solr in your environment. They are command line based; you can also use the *FireCURL* plugin to upload data through your Firefox browser.

The simple post tool is a command line tool for uploading the raw data to Apache Solr. You can simply run it on any file or type in your input through **STDIN** (which stands for **standard input stream**, that is, through keyboard) to load it in Apache Solr.

Understanding data import handlers

Apache Solr provides `DataImportHandler` to deal with this type of data source. With `DataImportHandler`, you can also load only the deltas, instead of the complete dataset again and again. Often, this can be set as an off-time scheduled job activity to minimize the impact of indexing on day-to-day work. In case of real-time updates, this activity should be scheduled with a fixed frequency.

One of the important steps before importing data from a database to Apache Solr is to configure the data source. A data source is pointed to the location where the data resides. In this case, it could be a relational database such as Oracle, MySQL, SQL Server, and HTTP URL.

A data source can be defined in `solrconfig.xml` or it can simply point to another file containing the configuration (in our case, `data-config.xml`). Each data source configuration has the `<dataSource>` and `<document>` elements. `<dataSource>` focuses more on establishing contact with data through different protocols such as JNDI, JDBC, and HTTP. Each `<document>` has `<entity>`. Each entity represents one dataset. An entity can contain entities or multiple fields. When the import handler is run, it generates a set of documents, containing multiple fields, which (after optionally being transformed in various ways) are sent to Solr for indexing. For an RDBMS data source, an entity is a view or table, which would be processed by one or more SQL statements to generate a set of rows (documents) with one or more columns (fields). You can create a custom data source by writing a class that extends `org.apache.solr.handler.dataimport.DataSource`. An import operation can be started from the following URL: `http://<host>:<port>/solr/dataimport?command=full-import`.

> There are two different modes available for importing data from a database through `DataImportHandler`. The full import mechanism is useful where it is required to read the data source snapshots at any given point of time. Delta import is similar to full import, but it offers the change of state of your data source to get reflected in Apache Solr. This import focuses on incremental updates and change detection.

Interacting with Solr through SolrJ

Apache Solr is a web application; it can be directly used by its customers for searching. The search interface can be modified and enhanced to work as an end user search tool for searching in an enterprise. Solr clients can directly access the Solr URL through HTTP to search and read data through various formats such as JSON and XML. Moreover, Apache Solr allows administration through these HTTP-based services. Queries are executed by generating a URL that Solr would understand.

SolrJ or SolrJava is a tool that can be used by your Java-based application to connect to Apache Solr for indexing. SolrJ allows Java wrappers and adaptors to communicate with Solr and translate its results to Java objects. Using SolrJ is much more convenient than using raw HTTP and JSON. Internally, SolrJ uses Apache HttpClient to send HTTP requests. It provides a user-friendly interface, hiding connection details from consumer applications. Using SolrJ, you can index your documents and execute your queries.

There are two major ways to do this; one is by using the EmbeddedSolrServer interface. If you are using Solr in an embedded application, this is the recommended interface for you. It does not use an HTTP-based connection. Here is the sample code:

```
System.setProperty("solr.solr.home", "/home/hrishi/work/scaling-solr/example/solr");
CoreContainer.Initializer initializer = new CoreContainer.Initializer();
CoreContainer coreContainer = initializer.initialize();
EmbeddedSolrServer server = new EmbeddedSolrServer(coreContainer, "");
ModifiableSolrParams params = new ModifiableSolrParams();
params.set("q", "Scaling");
QueryResponse response = server.query(params);
System.out.println("response = " + response);
```

The other way is to use the `HTTPSolrServer` interface, which talks with the Solr server through the HTTP protocol; this is suitable if you have a remote client-server-based application. It uses Apache commons HTTP client to connect to Solr. Here is the sample code for the same:

```
String url = "http://localhost:8983/solr";
SolrServer server = new HttpSolrServer( url );
ModifiableSolrParams params = new ModifiableSolrParams();
params.set("q", "Scaling");
QueryResponse response = server.query(params);
System.out.println("response = " + response);
```

You can use `ConcurrentUpdateSolrServer` for bulk uploads, whereas CloudSolrServer communicates with a Solr instance running in a cloud setup. SolrJ is available in the official Maven repository. You can simply add the following dependency to your `pom.xml` to use SolrJ:

```
<dependency>
        <artifactId>solr-solrj</artifactId>
        <groupId>org.apache.solr</groupId>
        <version>1.4.0</version>
        <type>jar</type>
        <scope>compile</scope>
</dependency>
```

To use EmbeddedSolrServer, you need to add the Solr-core dependency too:

```
<dependency>
        <artifactId>Solr-core</artifactId>
        <groupId>org.apache.Solr</groupId>
        <version>1.4.0</version>
        <type>jar</type>
        <scope>compile</scope>
</dependency>
```

Apache Solr also provides access to its services for different technologies, such as JavaScript, Python, and Ruby, given in the following table:

Technology	Interaction with Solr
JavaScript	Apache Solr can work with JavaScript in a client-server model through XMLHTTP/Standard Web Interface; you can use libraries such as ajax-Solr and SolrJS for interaction.
Ruby	For Ruby, there is a project called sunspot (`http://sunspot.github.io/`) that enables a Solr-powered search for Ruby Objects. You can also use DelRuby through APIs and SolrRuby libraries.

Technology	Interaction with Solr
PHP	PHP can talk with Solr in many ways. For example: PHP can consume Solr services through its handlers.
Java	Java can directly talk, with Solr through SolrJ APIs or through standard HTTP calls since Solr supports the HTTP interface.
Python	Python can utilize the Solr-Python Client API library to contact Solr for searching.
Perl	CPAN provides Solr libraries (`http://search.cpan.org/~garafola/Solr-0.03/`) for utilizing Solr search. However, you can also use a HTTP-based lightweight client to talk with Solr.
.NET	There are many implementations available for consuming Solr in a .Net-based application SolrNET (`https://github.com/mausch/SolrNet`) or Solr Contrib on CodePlex (`http://solrcontrib.codeplex.com/`).

Working with rich documents (Apache Tika)

Apache Tika is an SAX-based parser for extracting the metadata from different types of documents. Apache Tika uses the `org.apache.tika.parser.Parser` interface for extracting metadata and structured text content from various documents, by using the existing parser libraries. Apache Tika provides a single parse method with the following signature:

```
void parse(InputStream stream, ContentHandler handler, Metadata
metadata)
    throws IOException, SAXException, TikaException;
```

This method takes the stream of documents as input and generates an XHTML SAX event as the outcome. Thus, Tika provides a simple yet powerful interface for dealing with different types of documents. Apache Tika supports the following types of document formats: **Rich Text format (RTF)**, HTML, XHTML, Microsoft Office formats (Excel, Word, PowerPoint, Visio, and Outlook), **Portable Document Format (PDF)**, all types of text files, different types of compression formats (`zip`, `gzip`, `bzip`, `bzip2`, `tarball`, and so on), and audio formats (MP3, MIDI, and wave formats). The lyrics, title, and subject can be extracted from these formats.

Apache Tika will automatically attempt to determine the input document type (Word, PDF, and so on) and extract the content appropriately. Alternatively, you can specify the MIME type for Tika with the stream.type parameter. Apache Tika generates the XHTML stream through an SAX parser. Apache Solr then reacts to the SAX events by creating fields for indexing. Tika produces metadata information such as Title, Subject, and Author for the documents parsed.

Querying for information in Solr

We have already seen how Apache Solr effectively uses different request handlers to provide consumers with extensive ways of getting search results. Each Request Handler uses its own query parser, which extracts the parameters and their values from the query string and forms Lucene Query Objects. The standard query parser allows greater precision over search data; DisMaxQueryParser and Extended DisMaxQueryParser provide a Google-like searching syntax while searching. Depending upon which request handler called, the query syntax is changed. Let's look at some of the important terms:

Term	Meaning
`q?<string>`	The query string `<String>` can support wildcards (`*:*`); for example, `title:Scaling*`
`fl=id,book-name`	The field list that a search response will return
`sort=author asc`	Results/facets to be sorted by authors in an ascending order
`price[* TO 100]&rows=10&start=5`	Looks for price between 0 and 100; limits the result to 10 rows at a time, starting at the 5th matched result
`hl=true&hl.fl=name,features`	Enable highlighting by field list name and features
`&q=*:*&facet=true&facet.field=year`	Enables faceted search by the field "year"
`Publish-date:[NOW-1YEAR/DAY TO NOW/DAY]`	Published date between last year (same day) and today
`description:"Java sql"~10`	This is called proximity search. Searches for the descriptions containing Java and SQL in a single document with a proximity of 10 words maximum
`"open jdk" NOT "Sun JDK"`	Will search for an Open JDK term in the document
`&q=id:938099893&mlt=true`	Searches for a specific ID and similar results

[47]

Summary

This chapter was focused on making us aware of the Apache Solr enterprise search engine. We started with setting up Apache Solr, along with common problems and solutions, followed by the architecture and configuration of Apache Solr. We also looked at loading data in Apache Solr through different handlers. We explored how SolrJ can be used for interacting with Apache Solr. Now that we have a good understanding of Apache Hadoop and Apache Solr, the next step is to understand how to work with a distributed search with Apache Solr and Hadoop. In the next chapter, we will see how Apache Hadoop and Solr can complement each other.

3
Enabling Distributed Search using Apache Solr

With the growth of data for searching, it becomes necessary to scale up the performance of search applications, to cater to the increasing needs of indexing and searching quickly over large datasets. Distributed search can be used when a single index store becomes difficult to operate in terms of its size (large to fit in memory or disk). As more number of users start using enterprise search, single node searches have limitations in terms of response time and parallel sessions for users. For smaller data sizes, standalone search architecture performs better compared to distributed searches, due to single index availability. However, with the growth in the data size, its performance degrades eventually. The Distributed Search application increases the operation and maintenance cost. It also increases the complexity of overall landscape. However, with the scaling of information for searching, distributed search is the way to forward.

In *Chapter 2*, *Understanding Apache Solr*, we covered various aspects of Apache Solr, and looked at how it can be used in a search application. In this chapter, we will be looking at how to scale Apache Solr based search application, in order to work with a distributed environment. This chapter mainly focuses on using Apache Solr's capabilities to scale with growing data while keeping high performance. We will be covering the following topics in this chapter:

- Understanding Distributed Search and Scaling
- Working with Apache SolrCloud
- Sharding Algorithm and Fault Tolerance
- Apache Solr and Big Data: Integration with MongoDB

[49]

Understanding a distributed search

The decision to move to a distributed search from a standalone system should be driven by the needs of enterprises, because distributed search applications are not always efficient in terms of performance. In this section, we will focus on understanding distributed search patterns and how Apache Solr supports distributed search. There have been efforts made to enable Apache Solr work with Apache Hadoop platform in the past, and we will look at more details in coming chapters.

Distributed search patterns

There are two important functions of any enterprise search: creation of indexes and run-time searching on indexes. Any or either of these functions can run in distributed mode, depending upon the requirements from an enterprise. To utilize the distributed search, the indexing must be split into multiple shards and should be kept across multiple nodes of a distributed system.

> Sharding is a process of breaking one index into multiple logical units called "shards" across multiple records. In case of Solr, the results will be aggregated and returned.

The shard is a complete index, and it can be queried independently. The search application has to be smart enough to query multiple nodes, collect and combine the results and return to the client. The following architecture diagram depicts the overall scenario:

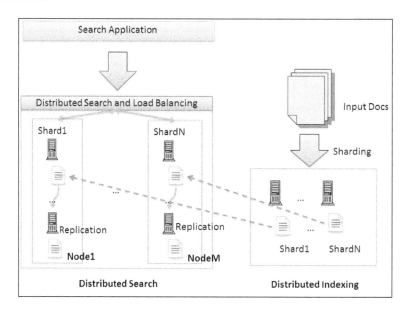

In distributed search, the index is divided among various shards, and they are stored locally on each node. Whenever a search query is fired by the user, load balancer effectively balances the load on each node, and the query is redirected to a node that tried to get the results. Some distributed searches such as Apache Solr do not use load balancer and, instead, each participating node handles the load balancing on its own by distributing the queries to respective shards. This pattern offers ample flexibility in terms of processing, due to multiple nodes participating in the cluster or distributed search setup. The results are collected and merged. Another aspect of distributed search is the replication. Using replication of enterprise search index, one can ensure high availability of instance. This kind of pattern is most suitable for situations where data size is finite and predictable, and the customer is looking for high availability features.

Based on the distributed architecture requirements, the following different types of enterprise distributed search implementation scenarios can be found:

- **Master/slave**: Where there is one master and multiple slaves. The Master is responsible for routing, and slaves perform the search on the index shards. This kind of setup is good for cases when users would like to have centralized control and routing strategy. This strategy has a risk of the master being a single point of failure. Earlier distributed Solr releases introduced master-slave configuration.

- **Multi-nodes**: All nodes are masters and index is divided among them. The search is assigned to any one of the nodes based on the load by balancer. This strategy is used by some of the most advanced distributed system, as it gets rid of the issue of master being the single point of failure. Current distributed Apache Solr supports multi-node clustering through SolrCloud. We are going to look at it in detail in this chapter.

- **Multi-tenant**: When multiple index/shards are part of enterprise search application. This is used by the service that provides search capabilities to different tenants. This can use multi-node or master-slave approach. In this approach, you can utilize same resources like CPU, memory, storage, and so on, for multiple tenants by means of sharing. This is particularly used in cloud-based deployments such as Amazon EC2, and private cloud deployments. Multi-tenant architecture enables organizations to focus their effort on one cluster due to its shared resources concept.

Apache Solr and distributed search

By design, Apache Lucene and Solr are designed to support large scale implementation. Apache Solr-based distributed environment is useful in the following instances:

- High sost of servers: When a Solr based server demands more resources for faster performance—an increase in memory or CPU is required that impacts the overall application cost.

- Index generation time: The incremental generation of indexes at faster speeds is an important part of the lifecycle of enterprise search. Distributed Solr can add faster performance to this.

- Large indexes: In cases when you have large indexes, a distribution of search index by means of partitioning adds a lot of value in terms of performance. Imagine a case when you are using Solr with terabytes of data (For Example: US patents database has terabytes of data): the index size would grow with more data getting in, and it would be difficult to fit on a single node.

At the same time, having your search distributed can address the following problems:

- There should be no single point of failure for your search engine. With effective replication of indexes, this can be achieved. This requires ensuring additional systems such as load balancer(For example: Nginx, haproxy) or DNS to provide high availability on top of your search application. Commercial Amazon ELBs (Elastic Load Balancing) provides such capabilities (More information: `http://aws.amazon.com/elasticloadbalancing/`).

- High Availability of the system in spite of multiple nodes failing. Thanks to high replication factor.

Apache Solr started support for distributed search since the release of 1.3 onwards. This approach had a straightforward way of creating shards and their replicas out of document index, keeping it on different nodes in the distributed system, and finally running search with parameter **shards** to run the search in a distributed manner. This system had its own limitations in terms of functionalities and feature support. We will not be covering the legacy of distributed search support of Apache Solr here: the information about this can be found on Solr wiki (`http://wiki.apache.org/solr/DistributedSearch` or `https://cwiki.apache.org/confluence/display/solr/Legacy+Scaling+and+Distribution`).

Lets start looking at Apache SolrCloud which is one of the most widely used distributed search for Apache Solr.

Working with SolrCloud

SolrCloud provides a new way to enable distributed enterprise search using a Apache Solr in enterprises. Previously, with the standard distributed Solr support, lot of the manual work had been automated by SolrCloud. With the introduction of SolrCloud, the manual steps like configuring `solr-config.xml` to talk with shards, adding documents to the shards, and so on, work became automatic. Unlike the traditional approach of master-slave based distributed Solr, SolrCloud provides a leader-replica-based approach as its implementation. SolrCloud runs on top of Apache ZooKeeper. First, let's understand the ZooKeeper.

Why ZooKeeper?

SolrCloud contains a cluster of nodes, which use Apache ZooKeeper to talk with each other. Apache ZooKeeper is responsible for maintaining co-ordination among various nodes. Besides co-ordinating among nodes, it also maintains configuration information, and group services to the distributed system. Due to its in-memory management of information; it offers the distributed co-ordination at high speed.

> Apache ZooKeeper itself is replicated over a set of nodes called an ensemble. They all form a set called ZooKeeper service. Each node that runs a ZooKeeper and stores its data is also called Znode.

Each ZooKeeper ensemble has one leader and many followers. The process of choosing a leader starts with the initialization of ZooKeeper cluster through election. Apache ZooKeeper nodes contain information related to distributed cluster, changes in the data, timestamp, and ACLs (Access Control List) as well as uploaded client information. ZooKeeper maintains a hierarchical metadata system similar to conventional UNIX file system. The following diagram depicts the structure of ZooKeeper in a distributed environment:

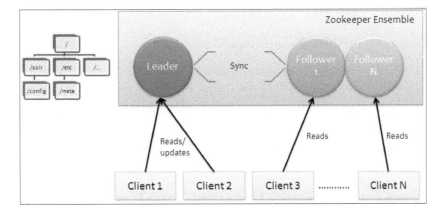

When the cluster is started, one of the nodes is elected as a leader. All others are followers. Each follower preserves the read-only copy of the leader's metadata in itself. Followers keep their metadata in sync with the leader by listening to the leader's atomic broadcast messages. Once broadcasted, the leader ensures that the majority of followers commit to the changes made, and informs the client of the transaction completion. This means that Apache ZooKeeper ensures **eventual consistency**. Clients are allowed to upload their own information on ZooKeeper and distribute it across the cluster. Clients can collect to followers for reading the information. ZooKeeper maintains a sequential track of updates through its transaction logs; hence it guarantees the **sequential updates** as they are received from different clients by the leader.

> Running ZooKeeper in standalone mode is convenient for development and testing. But in production, you should run ZooKeeper in replication. A replicated group of servers in the same application is called a quorum.

In case a leader fails, the next leader is chosen and clients are expected to connect to it. Apache Solr utilizes ZooKeeper to enable distributed capabilities. By default it provides the embedded ZooKeeper along with its default install. Apache ZooKeeper is being used by many distributed systems, including (in the past) Apache Hadoop.

The SolrCloud architecture

We have already seen the concepts of shards and indexing. It is important to understand some of the terminology used in SolrCloud. Unlike Apache ZooKeeper, SolrCloud has a similar concept of leaders and replicas. Let's assume we have to create a SolrCloud for documents database. Right now, document database has a total of three documents:

```
Document [1] = "what are you eating"
Document [2] = "are you eating pie"
Document [3] = "I like apple pie"
```

The inverted index for these documents will be:

```
what(1,1),are(1,2)(2,1),you(1,3)(2,2),eating(1,4)(2,3), pie(2,4)(3,4),
I(3,1),like(3,2), apple(3,3)
```

In this case, what (1, 1) represents word(document-identifier, offset). A **collection** is a complete set of indices in the SolrCloud cluster of nodes. So Solr will have the same information as mentioned in the preceding example of invested index.

Chapter 3

A **Shard Leader** in this case will be a piece of complete index. A **shard replica** contains a copy of the same shard. Together Shard Leader and Shard Replica form a complete **shard index or slice**. Let's say we divide the index into three shards, they will look like following:

```
Shard1: what(1,1),are(1,2)(2,1),you(1,3)(2,2)
Shard2: eating (1,4)(2,3), pie(2,4)(3,4)
Shard3: I (3,1),like(3,2), apple(3,3)
```

If we assume that all shards are replicated on two machines, each node participating in the SolrCloud will contain one or more shards and their replicas of the index. An example setup will look as shown in the following table:

Machine/VM	Solr Instance: Port*
M1	M1:8983/solr/ - Solr – Shard1
	M1:9983 – ZooKeeper – Leader
	M1:8883/solr/ - Solr – Shard3-Replica
M1	M1:8883/solr/ - Solr Shard2
	M1:9983 – ZooKeeper Follower
	M1:8883/solr/ - Solr Shard1-Replica
M2	M1:8983/solr/ - Solr Shard2-Replica
	M1:9983/solr/ - Solr Shard3

* The decision of follower/replica is made automatically by Apache ZooKeeper and Solr by default. In this case, Machine M1 holds two instances of Apache Solr at different ports, while machine M2 has a single instance.

A **Solr core** represents an instance of Apache Solr with complete configuration (such as `solrconfig.xml`, schema files, stop words, and others) that is required to run itself. In the preceding table, we can see a total of six Solr cores each with a machine running two different cores.

[55]

Enabling Distributed Search using Apache Solr

The organization and interaction between multiple Solr Cores and ZooKeeper can be seen in the following system context diagram:

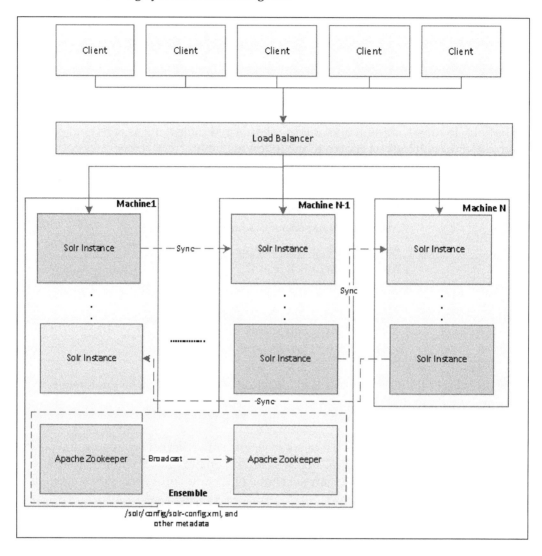

SolrCloud lets you create a cluster of Solr nodes, each of them running one or more collections. A collection holds one or more shards which are hosted on one or more (in case of replication) nodes. Any updates to any nodes participating in SolrCloud can in turn sync the rest of the nodes. SolrCloud uses Apache ZooKeeper in order to bring in distributed co-ordination and configuration among multiple nodes. This, in turn, enables near-real time searching on SolrCloud, due to an active sync of indexes. Apache ZooKeeper loads all the configuration files of Apache Solr in its own repository from file system and allows nodes to get access it in a distributed manner. With this, even if the instance goes away, the configuration will still be accessible to all other nodes. When a new core is introduced in SolrCloud, it registers with a ZooKeeper server, by sharing information regarding core, detailing how to contact. SolrCloud may run one or more collections.

SolrCloud does index distribution to the appropriate shard; it also takes care of distributing search across multiple shards. Search is possible with near-real time, after a document is committed. ZooKeeper provides load-balancing and failover to the Solr cluster, making the overall setup more robust. The index partitioning can be done in the following ways using Apache Solr:

- **Simple**: Use of hashing function to a fixed number of shards.
- **Prefix based**: Partitioning based on the document ID that is Red!12345, White! 22321. Red and White are example prefix names used for partitioning.
- **Custom**: Based on custom-defined partitioning, such as document creation time.

Building an enterprise distributed search using SolrCloud

In this section, we will try to build a Solr cluster using Apache Solr's SolrCloud. SolrCloud can be built for development and for production. Development would contain an easy, smaller version, whereas production would have a complex configuration.

Enabling Distributed Search using Apache Solr

Setting up SolrCloud for development

Development Environment typically does not require a fully-fledged production-level landscape. Developers can simply set up a single machine proxy cluster of nodes on their development server. Each Solr instance can run on any J2EE container like Jetty, Tomcat, or JBoss, and so on. In this mode, SolrCloud runs along with internal ZooKeeper provided by Solr installation. To start this, simply start your jetty server with the following command:

1. Download latest version of Apache Solr from `http://lucene.apache.org/solr/downloads.html`.

2. Unzip the instance, and go `$SOLR_HOME/example` directory.

3. Now run the following command:

   ```
   $ java -jar start.jar
   ```

4. Stop the server. This step of running Solr in a non-cloud mode is required to unpack the `jar` files required for SolrCloud.

5. Modify the schema and other configuration files, as per your requirements.

6. Now start the Solr in cluster configuration with the following command:

   ```
   java -DzkRun -DnumShards=2 -Dbootstrap_confdir=./solr/collection1/
   conf -Dcollection.configName=solrconf -jar start.jar
   ```

   Let's understand the different parameters in this process

Parameter	Description
zkRun	Runs an instance of embedded ZooKeeper as a part of Solr Server. Run this on one of the nodes, which will serve as a central node for all of the coordination.
collection.configName	Set the configuration to be used for Collection (Optional).
bootstrap_confdir=<dir-name>	The given directory name should contain the complete configuration for SolrCloud, which will include all of the configuration files such as solrconfig.xml, schema.xml, and others. When Solr runs, the configuration is loaded in ZooKeeper as the name given in collection.configName.
zkHost=<host>:<port>	This parameter points to the instance of ZooKeeper (ZooKeeper ensemble) containing the cluster state and configuration.
numShards=<number>	Solr cloud can be run on one or multiple indexes, the no. of shards denote no. of partitions to be carried out on these indexes.

[58]

Chapter 3

You are required to run this command only for the first time, in order to push the necessary configuration on ZooKeeper. From that point onwards, you can simply run

```
java -DzkRun -jar start.jar
```

7. You will find on the console, the ZooKeeper selection for a leader, followed by all the configurations getting loaded in ZooKeeper. Apache ZooKeeper stores the metadata at $SOLR_HOME/example/solr/zoo_data/

8. You can also validate the Solr configuration loaded in ZooKeeper by going to $SOLR_HOME\ example\scripts\cloud-scripts and running the following command to get schema.xml from the ZooKeeper metadata store:

```
zkcli.sh -zkhost localhost:9983 -cmd get /configs/solrconf/schema.
xml
```

9. Now create another Solr node, either by copying $SOLR_HOME/example directory to $SOLR_CORE/example1, or creating another instance from downloaded solr.zip. You can do this on the same machine, or on a different machine.

10. Now run the following command:

```
java -Djetty.port=8888 -DzkHost=myhost:9983 -jar start.jar
```

[59]

Enabling Distributed Search using Apache Solr

11. This will start another node with shard. Now access `http://localhost:8983/solr/#/~cloud` and, you will find the shards, with the collection seeing how they are linked, as shown in the following screenshot:

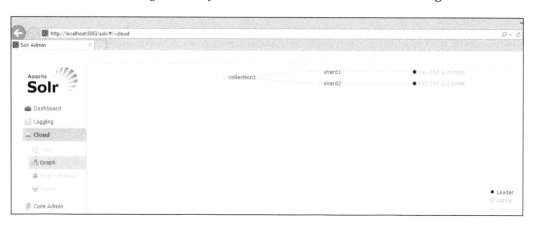

In the screenshot, Apache Solr administration user interface introspects among the nodes participating in the cloud, and provides a graphical representation of leaders, active status. By default, cluster continues in round robin fashion adding shards, followed by replicas as-and-when a node is added. The Round Robin algorithm ensures equal sharding for all of the nodes that are participating (for more information visit `http://en.wikipedia.org/wiki/Round-robin_scheduling`). Replicas are assigned automatically, unless their role is stated specifically by passing parameter `-DshardId=1`.

Setting up SolrCloud for production

To run a SolrCloud instance with multi-node, it is recommended that you run it by using a separate ZooKeeper instead of using with an embedded ZooKeeper. A fully distributed setup will require the Apache ZooKeeper ensemble setup. Let's set up Apache ZooKeeper first using the following steps:

1. Download latest version of Apache ZooKeeper from `http://zookeeper.apache.org/releases.html#download`.
2. Copy and unzip it on all the nodes that are expected to participate in ZooKeeper ensemble.
3. Create a directory `$ZK_HOME/zkdata`, and run the following command:

   `$cat 1 > $ZK_HOME/zkdata/myid`

   The number here denotes the ID of the server. Similarly, all the participating nodes should be assigned a unique identifier in this fashion.

Chapter 3

4. Now create `$ZK_HOME/conf/zoo.cfg` with the following entries:

```
dataDir=$ZK_HOME/zkdata
server.1=node1:2888:3888
server.2=node2:2888:3888
clientPort=2181
tickTime=2000
syncLimit=5
initLimit=10
```

   Here, `server.N` provides a list of servers that participate in ZooKeeper Service. The ports: `2888` and `3888` in case of `server.1` denote port for communication with peers, and port for leader selection respectively. The `initLimit` entry is the maximum time in which ZooKeeper in quorum should connect to the leader. The `syncLimit` entry denotes the maximum time of sync with the leader. While `initLimit` and `syncLimit` are units of tick, `tickTime` denotes the time of tick. In this case, `tickTime` is `2000` milliseconds, which means that the server will perform syncing every 10000 ms. In this case, ZooKeeper will run a replicated mode, that is, `node1` and `node2` are replicated.

5. You need to make sure that `node1` and `node2` entries are the names of the nodes, and ensure that your host or DNS resolves them to appropriate IP addresses. You can find the host file in `/etc/host` in Unix, and in Windows you will find it at `%System Root%\system32\drivers\etc\hosts`.

6. Run all ZooKeeper nodes by running:

   `$ZK_HOME/bin/zkServer.cmd or zkServer.sh`

7. Check if the instance is available by connecting to ZooKeeper server. You can do this by running the following command:

   `bin\zkCli.cmd -server node1:2181`

8. Now connect to ZooKeeper by running:

   `[zk:] connect node1:2181`

9. Now, it will show that it is connected in the next command prompt.

   `[zk: node1:2181(CONNECTED) 2]`

10. Run ZooKeeper client commands, such as `ls` (list directory) to validate the current metadata of Apache ZooKeeper, you can enter the following command in shell:

    `[zk: node1:2181(CONNECTED) 2] ls`

Enabling Distributed Search using Apache Solr

You may also choose to configure logger for ZooKeeper in the `log4j.properties` file. This will in turn help you quickly detect any find out issues for the initial start.

```
23    zookeeper.root.logger=INFO, CONSOLE
24    zookeeper.console.threshold=INFO
25    zookeeper.log.dir=/var/hrishi/zookeeper/log/
26    zookeeper.log.file=zookeeper.log
27    zookeeper.log.threshold=DEBUG
28    zookeeper.tracelog.dir=/var/hrishi/zookeeper/trace-log/
29    zookeeper.tracelog.file=zookeeper_trace.log
```

Now your Apache ZooKeeper ensemble is set up, we can configure Apache Solr in the recommended setup for production using jetty. In case of Apache Tomcat or any other container, the parameters are to be passed through the standard J2EE parameter container:

1. You need to follow the steps you performed while setting up the development environment. Download and unzip the instance at every node that is participating in the SolrCloud.

2. Now identify the number of shards, and accordingly set the parameters. Start with on one of these node:

```
java -DnumShards=2 -Dbootstrap_confdir=./solr/collection1/conf
-Dcollection.configName=testconf -DzkHost=node1:2181,node2:2181
-jar start.jar
```

Please note that all the ZooKeeper nodes in the replicated phase have to be passed to `-DzkHost` parameters in the comma separated manner.

3. Once this server is up, the other nodes can be started using the following command:

```
java -Djetty.port=<your-choice-of-port> -DzkHost=<zkeeper-
leader>:2183 -jar start.jar
```

[62]

Chapter 3

Once the nodes are started, you can validate them through administration user interface. Solr Admin provides additional information. The Tree view provides directory browsing of Cloud based configuration, which, is part of ZooKeeper, and you can access it by browsing `http://localhost:8983/solr/#/~cloud?view=tree`.

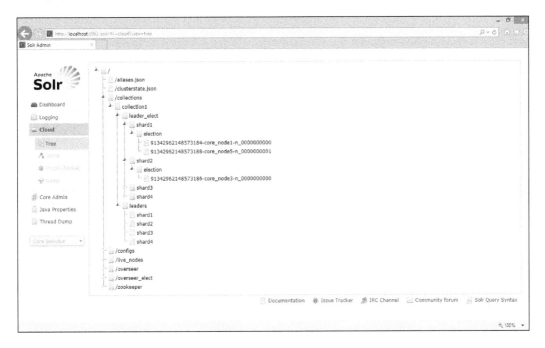

The admin UI shows information related to cluster, the current shards along with leaders, status of a cluster and Solr cluster configuration. You can also use the utility zkCLI (ZooKeeper command-line interface) to read/write the data to and from ZooKeeper store.

>
> **Downloading the example code**
> You can download the example code files for all Packt books you have purchased from your account at `http://www.packtpub.com`. If you purchased this book elsewhere, you can visit `http://www.packtpub.com/support` and register to have the files e-mailed directly to you.

[63]

Adding a document to SolrCloud

To add a document in Solr, you can simply choose any node part of your cluster and run the following command:

```
curl http://node1:8983/solr/update/json -H 'Content-type:application/json' -d
'
[
{"id" : "1", "text" : "This is a test document"}]'
```

You can also load files from the example directory as shown here:

```
curl http://node1:8983/solr/update/csv --data-binary @books.csv -H 'Content-type:text/plain; charset=utf-8'
```

This command uploads CSV file. Once this is complete, validate the uploaded document by running the query through browser/administration window, or simply typing in browser `http://localhost:8983/solr/collection1/select?q=*%3A*&wt=json&indent=true`.

When `node1` in the Solr cluster receives a request for indexing the document, if the document is a replica, it forwards it to the leader of the shard. Each leader performs hashing on the document ID, based on its prefix or automatically, and if the leader does not own the responsibility of that shard, it has to forward it to the leader of the shard. Once the correct leader receives the document, it updates its transactional log, and forwards the document to its replica for replication. When the document is first received, it is assigned version ID, and the leader first tries to see if it has a higher version. If it does, then the leader will simply ignore the uploaded document.

> The Solr Transactional Log is an append-only log of write operations per node in a cluster. Solr records all the write operations before the write commit, and marks it post commit. If the indexing process is stopped for some reason, next time, Solr will first review transaction logs, and then completes the pending indexing.

Creating shards, collections, and replicas in SolrCloud

You can create shards, collections, and their replicas on SolrCloud through the web-based handlers provided by Solr, by uploading them using CURL utility. Now, let's try an exercise of creating a distributed search index (shard) with replicas on one collection for SolrCloud. First, we need to start with the creation of a collection (that is, clusterCollection) assuming the replication of 3, and max shards per node = 2:

```
curl 'http://node1:8983/solr/admin/collections?action=CREATE&name=clusterCollection&numShards=3&replicationFactor=3&maxShardsPerNode=2'
```

This will create a collection with name clusterCollection on Solr. We have already linked its configuration through ZooKeeper earlier.

Now, let's create replicas of the shards by running the following command (this command has to run for each replica that you intend to create in your Solr instance).

```
curl 'http://node1:8983/solr/admin/cores?action=CREATE&name=shardA-Replica1&collection=clusterCollection&shard=shardA'
```

```
curl 'http://node2:8983/solr/admin/cores?action=CREATE&name=shardB-Replica2&collection=clusterCollection&shard=shardB'
```

The following example shows how the admin UI will show the shard distribution of your indexes:

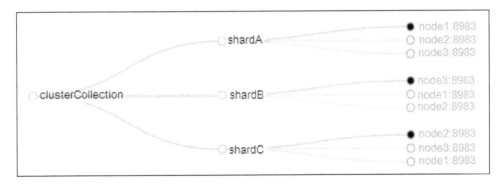

Enabling Distributed Search using Apache Solr

Now the documents can directly be posted to any of the nodes hosting Solr index. The following example shows uploading of default documents shipped with Solr on this cloud instance:

```
cd $SOLR_HOME/example/exampledocs/
java -Durl=http://node1:8983/solr/clusterCollection/update -jar post.
jar ipod_video.xml
java -Durl=http://node2:8983/solr/clusterCollection/update -jar post.
jar monitor.xml
```

You can simply verify this it by accessing Solr instance with wildcard query:

```
http://node1:8983/solr/clusterCollection/select?q=*:*
```

Common problems and resolutions

Now the installation is successful, let's try to address some of the common problems and their solutions that you may face during set up:

- **I have been using SolrCloud for a long time, and today when I ran it, it showed me some of the old nodes in the current cluster landscape. How do I fix this?**

  This can be fixed by cleaning ZooKeeper metadata. However, first you need to back-up the existing ZooKeeper metadata using zkCLI command (`get`/`getfile` calls). Once you back-up the ZooKeeper, shut down all the instances, and rename `$SOLR_HOME/example/solr/zoo_data` directory to a different name, and then restart SolrCloud, and ZooKeeper. This will recreate the ZooKeeper configuration again and add configuration directories. You can validate the new cluster configuration of Apache ZooKeeper by running zkCLI with

  ```
  [zk: node1:2181(CONNECTED) 4] get /clusterstate.json
  ```

Chapter 3

This will show the complete details of the cluster. You can also validate this through the administration console by browsing the `/clusterstate.json` file as shown in the following screenshot:

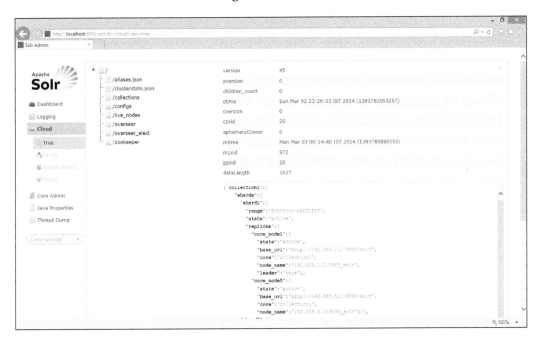

- **I am getting lot of exceptions from Solr with connection time out as the error description.**

    Since the connections are timing out, one possibility is that the leader itself is going down, or the responses are slow due to network latency. This can be fixed by increasing the timeout of Apache ZooKeeper. The `zoo.cfg` file contains a tick time (usually 2 seconds): this should not be touched, instead modify property `zkClientTimeout` in `solrconfig.xml` to work with more ticks for ZooKeeper.

- **I have a single node Solr instance with information indexed as of now, can I migrate this index to SolrCloud anyway?**

    There is no support for this kind of problem in Apache Solr (Version 4.6), so in this case, you need to re-parse all the documents, and re-index them one more time.

[67]

Sharding algorithm and fault tolerance

We have already seen the sharding, collection and replicas. In this section we will look at some of the important aspects of sharding, and how it plays a role in scalability and high availability. The strategy for creating new shards is highly dependent upon the hardware and the shard size. Let's say, you have two machines M1 & M2, of, the same configuration, each with one shard. Shard A is loaded with 1 million index documents, and shard B is loaded with 100 documents. When a query is fired, the query response to any Solr queries is determined by the query response of slowest node (in this case shard A). Hence having a shard with near to equal shard sizes can perform better in this case.

Document Routing and Sharding

Typically, when any enterprise search is deployed, the size of documents to be indexed keeps growing over time. Since SolrCloud provides a way to create a cluster of Solr nodes running on index shards, it becomes feasible to scale up the enterprise search infrastructure with time. However, as the shard size grows, it becomes difficult to manage them on a single shard. SolrCloud can be started with `numOfShards` controlling how many shards are run in the cloud. To route the newly indexed documents, take a look at the following flowchart:

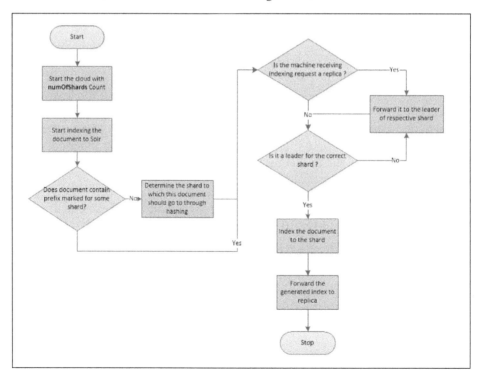

When a Solr instance is started, it firstly registers itself with ZooKeeper, creating Ephemeral Node or Znodes. A ZooKeeper provides a shared hierarchical namespace for processes to co-ordinate with each other. The namespace consists of the data registered, called Znodes. Apache Solr provides you with two ways to distribute Solr documents across shards. Auto-sharding distributes the documents automatically through its own hashing algorithm. Each shard is allocated with a range for hashing, and it can be seen in /clusterstate.json as shown in the following screenshot:

```
{"collection1":{
    "shards":{
      "shard1":{
        "range":"80000000-ffffffff",
        "state":"active",
        "replicas":{"core_node1":{
            "state":"active",
            "base_url":"http://192.168.2.4:8983/solr",
            "core":"collection1",
            "node_name":"192.168.2.4:8983_solr",
            "leader":"true"}}},
      "shard2":{
        "range":"0-7fffffff",
        "state":"active",
        "replicas":{}}},
    "maxShardsPerNode":"1",
    "router":{"name":"compositeId"},
    "replicationFactor":"1",
    "autoCreated":"true"}}
```

Another way of distributing the document across a shard is to use custom sharding. With custom sharding, client applications that pass documents for indexing to Apache Solr are primarily responsible for placing them in a shard. Each document has a unique ID attribute, and a shard key can be prefixed to this ID, for example: shard1!docId55. The ! operator acts as a separator. Custom Sharding helps users in influence the storage for his document indexes.

[69]

Enabling Distributed Search using Apache Solr

Users can choose various strategies for distributing the shards across different nodes for efficient usage. Similarly, a query can be performed on a specific shard (instead of a complete index) by passing `shard.keys=shard1!,shard2!` as a query parameter. These features enable Apache Solr to work in a multi-tenancy environment, or as a regional distributed search. You can also spread tenants across multiple shards by introducing another prefix for the unique ID. The syntax for this looks like:

```
Shard_key/number!doc_id
```

Shard splitting

The feature of Shard splitting was introduced in Apache Solr 4.3. It is designed to work with Apache Solr's auto-sharding. It allows users to split shards without breaking the search runtime or even the indexing. A shard can be split into two by running the following URL on your browser:

```
http://localhost:8983/solr/admin/collections?collection=collection1&s
hard=[shard_name]&action=SPLITSHARD
```

As you split the shards, the average query performance tends to slow down. The call to SPLITSHARD will create two new shards (shard1_1, and shard1_2 out of shard1) as shown in the following screenshot:

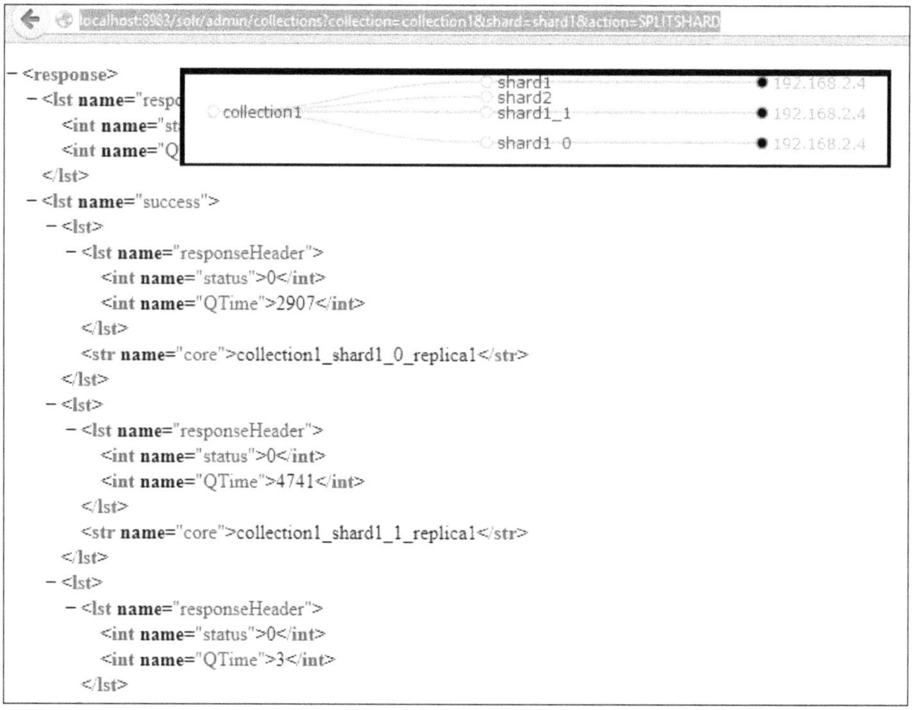

Chapter 3

The numbers of documents are divided equally across these two sub-shards. Once the split is complete, shard1 will be made inactive. The new subshards get created in construction state, and the index updates on shard start getting forwarded to new subshards. Once the splitting is complete, the parent shard becomes inactive. The old shard can be deleted by calling DELETESHARD in the following way:

```
http://localhost:8983/solr/admin/
collections?collection=collection1&shard=shard1&action=DELETESHARD
```

With large index sizes, the search performance can become slow. Auto-sharding in Solr lets you start with a fixed number of shards, and shard splitting, offers an easy way to reduce the size of each shard across Solr cores as the index size grows.

> Although the parent shard is inactive, Solr Admin UI does not become aware of the states, and shows the parent shard in green (active) state.

Load balancing and fault tolerance in SolrCloud

SolrCloud provides built-in load balancing capabilities to its clients. So, when a request is sent to one of the servers, it is re-directed to the respective leader to get all the information. If your client application is Java based, you can rely on CloudSolrServer and LbHttpSolrServer (load balanced HTTP server) classes of SolrJ to perform indexing and search across SolrCloud. CloudSolrServer will load balance queries across all operational servers automatically. The Java code through SolrJ for searching on SolrCloud is as follows:

```
CloudSolrServer server = new CloudSolrServer("localhost:9983");
server.setDefaultCollection("collection1");
SolrQuery solrQuery = new SolrQuery("*.*");
QueryResponse response = server.query(solrQuery);
SolrDocumentList dList = response.getResults();
for (int i = 0; i < dList.getNumFound(); i++)
{
   for (Map.Entry mE : dList.get(i).entrySet())
     {
       System.out.println(mE.getKey() + ":" + mE.getValue());
     }
}
```

[71]

Enabling Distributed Search using Apache Solr

Fault tolerance is the ability to keep the system functions working with degraded support, even in the case of failure of a system components. Fault tolerance in SolrCloud is managed at different levels.

Since SolrCloud performs its own load balancing, a call to any one of the nodes participating in the cloud can be made. The applications that do not rely on a Java-based client may require a load balancer to fire queries. The intent of the load balancer is not to balance the load, but enable the removal of a single point of failure for the calling party. So in case of a failure of node1, the load balancer can forward the query to node2, thus enabling fault tolerance in Apache Solr.

When a search request is fired on SolrCloud, the request gets executed on all leaders of that shard (unless a user chooses a shard in their query). If one of the nodes is failing to respond to a Solr query due to an error, the wait for the final search result can be avoided by enabling support for partial results. This support can be enabled by passing `shards.tolerant=true`. This read-side fault tolerance ensures that the system returns the results, in spite of the unavailability of the node.

Apache Solr also supports write-side fault tolerance that makes the instance durable, even in the instance of power failures, restarts, JVM crash, and so on. Each node participating in Solr maintains a transaction log, tracking all the changes to the node. This logging helps Solr node to recover in case of failures or interruption during the indexing operation.

Apache Solr and Big Data – integration with MongoDB

In an enterprise, data is generated from all the software that is participating in day-to-day operations. This data has different formats, and bringing in this data for big-data processing requires a storage system that is flexible enough to accommodate a data with varying data models. A NoSQL database, by its design, is best suited for this kind of storage requirements. One of the primary objectives of NoSQL is horizontal scaling, that is, the P in CAP theorem, but this works at the cost of sacrificing Consistency or Availability. Visit `http://en.wikipedia.org/wiki/CAP_theorem` to understand more about CAP theorem.

What is NoSQL and how is it related to Big Data?

As we have seen, data models for NoSQL differ completely from that of a relational database. With the flexible data model, it becomes very easy for developers to quickly integrate with the NoSQL database, and bring in large sized data from different data sources. This makes the NoSQL database ideal for Big Data storage, since it demands that different data types be brought together under one umbrella. NoSQL also has different data models, like KV store, document store and Big Table storage.

In addition to flexible schema, NoSQL offers scalability and high performance, which is again one of the most important factors to be considered while running big data. NoSQL was developed to be a distributed type of database. When traditional relational stores rely on the high computing power of CPUs and the high memory focused on a centralized system, NoSQL can run on your low-cost, commodity hardware. These servers can be added or removed dynamically from the cluster running NoSQL, making the NoSQL database easier to scale. NoSQL enables most advanced features of a database, like data partitioning, index sharding, distributed query, caching, and so on.

Although NoSQL offers optimized storage for big data, it may not be able to replace the relational database. While relational databases offer transactional (ACID), high CRUD, data integrity, and a structured database design approach, which are required in many applications, NoSQL may not support them. Hence it is most suited for Big Data where there is less possibility of need for data to be transactional.

MongoDB at glance

MongoDB is one of the popular NoSQL databases, (just like Cassandra). MongoDB supports the storing of any random schemas in the document oriented storage of its own. MongoDB supports the JSON-based information pipe for any communication with the server. This database is designed to work with heavy data. Today, many organizations are focusing on utilizing MongoDB for various enterprise applications.

MongoDB provides high availability and load balancing. Each data unit is replicated and the combination of a data with its copes is called a replica set. Replicas in MongoDB can either be primary or secondary. Primary is the active replica, which is used for direct read-write operations, while the secondary replica works like a backup for the primary. MongoDB supports searches by field, range queries, and regular expression searches. Queries can return specific fields of documents and also include user-defined JavaScript functions. Any field in a MongoDB document can be indexed. More information about MongoDB can be read at https://www.mongodb.org/.

The data on MongoDB is eventually consistent. Apache Solr can be used to work with MongoDB, to enable database searching capabilities on a MongoDB-based data store. Unlike Cassandra, where the Solr indexes are stored directly in Cassandra through solandra, MongoDB integration with Solr brings in the indexes in the Solr-based optimized storage.

There are various ways in which the data residing in MongoDB can be analyzed and searched. MongoDB's replication works by recording all operations made on a database in a log file, called the oplog (operation log). Mongo's oplog keeps a rolling record of all operations that modify the data stored in your databases. Many of the implementers suggest reading this log file using a standard file IO program to push the data directly to Apache Solr, using CURL, SolrJ. Since oplog is a collection of data with an upper limit on maximum storage, it is feasible to synch such querying with Apache Solr. Oplog also provides tailable cursors on the database. These cursors can provide a natural order to the documents loaded in MongoDB, thereby, preserving their order. However, we are going to look at a different approach. Let's look at the schematic following diagram:

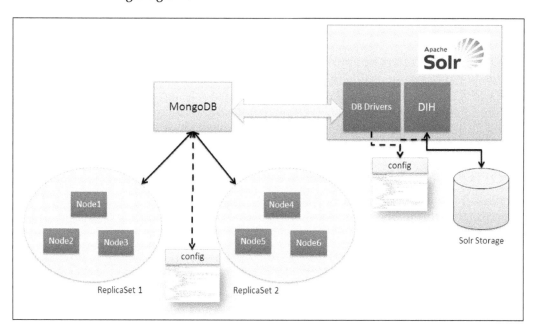

In this case, MongoDB is exposed as a database to Apache Solr through the custom database driver. Apache Solr reads MongoDB data through the DataImportHandler, which in turns calls the JDBC-based MongoDB driver for connecting to MongoDB and running data import utilities. Since MongoDB supports replica sets, it manages the distribution of data across nodes. It also supports Sharding just like Apache Solr.

Installing MongoDB

To install MongoDB in your development environment, please follow the following steps:

1. Download the latest version of MongoDB from `https://www.mongodb.org/downloads` for your supported operating system.
2. Unzip the zipped folder.
3. MongoDB comes up with a default set of different command-line components and utilities:
   - `bin/mongod`: The database process.
   - `bin/mongos`: Sharding controller.
   - `bin/mongo`: The database shell (uses interactive JavaScript).
4. Now, create a directory for MongoDB, which it will use for user data creation and management, and run the following command to start the single node server:

   ```
   $ bin/mongod –dbpath <path to your data directory> --rest
   ```

   In this case, `--rest` parameter enables support for simple rest APIs that can be used for getting the status.
5. Once the server is started, access `http://localhost:28017` from your favorite browser, you should be able to see following administration status page:

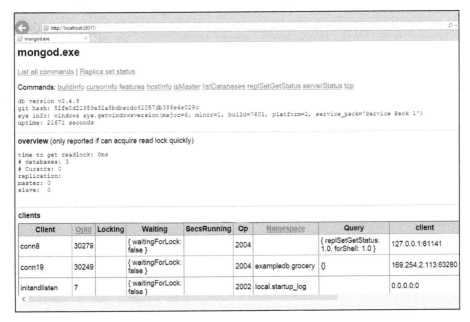

Enabling Distributed Search using Apache Solr

Now that you have successfully installed MongoDB, try loading a sample data set from the book on MongoDB by opening a new command-line interface. Change the directory to $MONGODB_HOME and run the following command:

```
$ bin/mongoimport --db solr-test --collection zips --file "<file-dir>/
samples/zips.json"
```

Please note that the database name is solr-test. You can see the stored data using the MongoDB-based CLI by running the following set of commands from your shell:

```
$ bin/mongo
MongoDB shell version: 2.4.9
connecting to: test
Welcome to the MongoDB shell.
For interactive help, type "help".
For more comprehensive documentation, see
        http://docs.mongodb.org/
Questions? Try the support group
        http://groups.google.com/group/mongodb-user
> use test
Switched to db test
> show dbs
exampledb       0.203125GB
local   0.078125GB
test    0.203125GB
> db.zips.find({city:"ACMAR"})
{ "city" : "ACMAR", "loc" : [  -86.51557,   33.584132 ], "pop" : 6055,
"state" :"AL", "_id" : "35004" }
```

Congratulations! MongoDB is installed successfully

[76]

Chapter 3

Creating Solr indexes from MongoDB

To run MongoDB as a database, you will need a JDBC driver built for MongoDB. However, the Mongo-JDBC driver has certain limitations, and it does not work with the Apache Solr DataImportHandler. So, I have extended Mongo-JDBC to work under the Solr-based DataImportHandler. The project repository is available at https://github.com/hrishik/solr-mongodb-dih. Let's look at the setting-up procedure for enabling MongoDB based Solr integration:

1. You may not require a complete package from the `solr-mongodb-dih` repository, but just the `jar` file. This can be downloaded from https://github.com/hrishik/solr-mongodb-dih/tree/master/sample-jar. The compiled `jar` file is also available with this book for easy access. You will also need the following additional `jar` files:

   ○ `jsqlparser.jar`

   ○ `mongo.jar`

   These jars are made available with this book as well as, and you will find them in the `lib` directory of the `solr-mongodb-dih` repository.

2. In your Solr setup, copy these `jar` files into the library path, that is, the `$SOLR_WAR_LOCATION/WEB-INF/lib` folder. Alternatively, point your container classpath variable to link them up.

3. Using simple Java source code `DataLoad.java` (link https://github.com/hrishik/solr-mongodb-dih/blob/master/examples/DataLoad.java), populate the database with some sample schema and tables that you will use to load in Apache Solr.

4. Now create a data source file (`data-source-config.xml`) as follows:

```
<dataConfig>
   <dataSource name="mongod" type="JdbcDataSource" driver="com.
mongodb.jdbc.MongoDriver" url="mongodb://localhost/solr-test"/>
   <document>
     <entity name="nameage" dataSource="mongod" query="select name,
price from grocery">
         <field column="name" name="name"/>
         <field column="name" name="id"/>
         <!-- other files -->
     </entity>
   </document>
</dataConfig>
```

[77]

Enabling Distributed Search using Apache Solr

5. Copy the `solr-dataimporthandler-*.jar` from your `contrib` directory to a container/application library path.

6. Modify `$SOLR_COLLECTION_ROOT/conf/solr-config.xml` with DIH entry:

```
<!-- DIH Starts -->
<requestHandler name="/dataimport" class="org.apache.solr.
handler.dataimport.DataImportHandler">
    <lst name="defaults">
      <str name="config"><path to config>/data-source-config.xml</
str>
    </lst>
</requestHandler>
  <!-- DIH ends -->
```

7. Once this configuration is done, you are ready to test it out. Access `http://localhost:8983/solr/dataimport?command=full-import` from your browser to run the full import on Apache Solr, where you will see that your import handler has successfully ran, and has loaded the data in Solr store, as shown in the following screenshot:

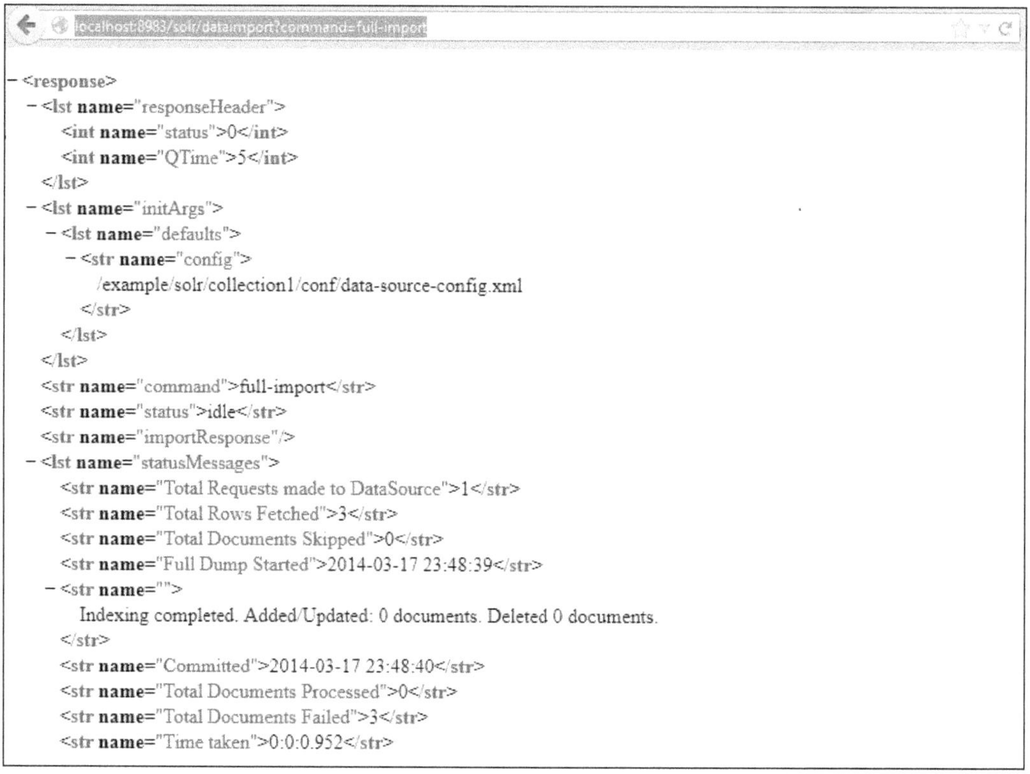

[78]

You can validate the content created by your new MongoDB DIH by accessing the **Solr Admin** page, and running a query:

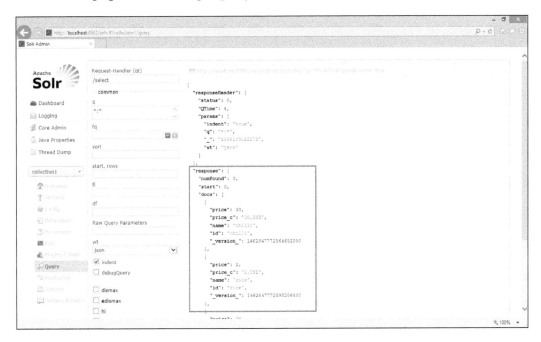

Using this connector, you can perform operations for full-import on various data elements. Since MongoDB is not a relational database, it does support join queries. However, it supports selects, order by, and so on.

Summary

In this chapter, we have understood the distributed aspects of any enterprise search. We understood distributed search patterns, and how Apache Solr can be used as a distributed search. We started working with Apache SolrCloud, by understanding its architecture, and building a SolrCloud instance of development and production. We also looked at sharding strategies and fault tolerance. Finally, we went through Apache Solr and MongoDB together. In the coming chapter, we will see how Apache Hadoop and Solr can complement each other, alongside the various implementations of Solr with Hadoop.

4
Big Data Search Using Hadoop and Its Ecosystem

Sometime back, Gartner (http://www.gartner.com/newsroom/id/2304615) published an executive program survey report, which revealed that big data and analytics are among the top 10 business priorities for CIOs; similarly, analytics and BI are also at the top of CIO's Technical Priorities. Big data presents three major concerns for any organization: namely the storage of big data, data access or querying, and data analytics. Apache Hadoop provides an excellent implementation framework for the organizations looking to solve these problems. Similarly, there is other software that provides efficient storage and access to big data, such as Apache Cassandra and R Statistical. In this chapter, we will explore the possibilities of Apache Solr in working with big data.

We have already discussed a scaling search with SolrCloud in the previous chapters. In this chapter, we will be focusing on the following topics:

- Understanding NoSQL
- Working with Solr HDFS Connector
- Big data Search using Katta
- Solr 1045 Patch: Map Side Indexing
- Solr 1301 Patch: Reduce Side Indexing
- Distributed Search using Apache Blur
- Apache Solr and Cassandra
- Scaling Solr through Storm
- Advanced Analytics with Solr

[81]

Understanding NoSQL

Traditional relational databases allow users to define a strict data structure, and use an SQL-based querying mechanism. NoSQL databases, rather than confining users to define the data structures, allow an open database with which they can store any kind of data and retrieve it by running queries that are not SQL based. In an enterprise, data is generated from all the software used in day-to-day operations. This data has different formats, and bringing in this data for big-data processing requires for a storage system that is flexible enough, to accommodate data with varying data models. The NoSQL database, by design is best suited for such storage.

> The CAP theorem or Brewer's theorem talks about distributed consistency. It states that it is impossible to achieve all of the following in a distributed system:
> - **Consistency**: Every client sees the most recently updated data state.
> - **Availability**: The distributed system functions as expected, even if there are node failures.
> - **Partition tolerance**: Intermediate network failure among nodes does not impact system functioning.
>
> Achieving all three of these capabilities is a difficult task, so most databases focus on achieving any two. You can read more information on the CAP theorem at http://en.wikipedia.org/wiki/CAP_theorem.

One of the primary objectives of NoSQL is horizontal scaling, that is, achieving the P in the CAP theorem at the cost of sacrificing Consistency or Availability. As we have seen, data models for NoSQL differ completely from those of relational databases. With the flexible data model, it becomes very easy for developers to quickly integrate the NoSQL database and bring in heavy data from different data sources. This makes NoSQL databases ideal for big data storage, since it demands different data types to be brought together under one umbrella.

In addition to flexible schema, NoSQL offers scalability and high performance, which is again one of the most important factors to be considered while running big data.

Working with the Solr HDFS connector

Apache Solr can utilize HDFS for indexing and storing its indices on the Hadoop system. It does not utilize a MapReduce-based framework for indexing. The following diagram shows the interaction pattern between Solr and HDFS. You can read more details about Apache Hadoop at http://hadoop.apache.org/docs/r2.4.0/.

Chapter 4

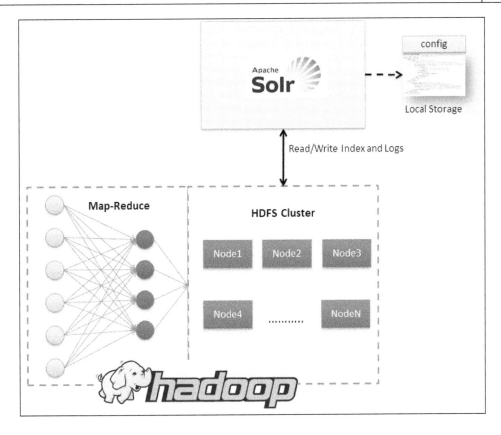

Let's understand how this can be done.

1. To start with, the first and most important task is getting Apache Hadoop set up on your machine (proxy node configuration), or setting up a Hadoop cluster. You can download the latest Hadoop tarball or zip from http://hadoop.apache.org. The newer generation Hadoop uses advanced MapReduce (also known as YARN).

2. Based on the requirement, you can set up a single node (Documentation: http://hadoop.apache.org/docs/r<version>/hadoop-project-dist/hadoop-common/SingleCluster.html) or a cluster (Documentation: http://hadoop.apache.org/docs/r<version>/hadoop-project-dist/hadoop-common/ClusterSetup.html).

3. Typically, you will be required to set up the Hadoop environment and modify different configurations (yarn-site.xml, hdfs-site.xml, master, slaves, and others). Once it is set up, restart the Hadoop cluster.

[83]

Big Data Search Using Hadoop and Its Ecosystem

4. Once Hadoop is setup, verify the installation of Hadoop by accessing `http://host:port/cluster`. You will see the following Hadoop cluster status:

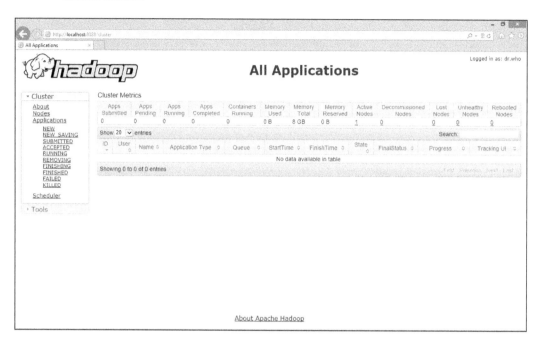

5. Now, using the HDFS command, create a folder in HDFS to keep your Solr index and Solr logs :

   ```
   $ $HADOOP_HOME/bin/hdfs.sh dfs -mkdir /Solr
   ```
   ```
   $ $HADOOP_HOME/bin/hdfs.sh dfs -mkdir /Solr-logs
   ```

   This call will create folders in the root folder, that is , /, on HDFS. You can verify these by running:

   ```
   $ $HADOOP_HOME/bin/hdfs.sh dfs -ls /
   ```

   ```
   Found 2 items
   drwxr-xr-x   - hrishi supergroup          0 2014-05-11 11:29 /Solr
   drwxr-xr-x   - hrishi supergroup          0 2014-05-11 11:27 /Solr-logs
   ```

   You can also browse the folder structure by accessing `http://<host>:50070/`.

[84]

6. Once the folders are created, the next step will be to point Apache Solr to run with Hadoop HDFS. This can be done by passing JVM arguments for DirectoryFactory. If you are running Solr on a jetty, you can use the following command:

   ```
   java -Dsolr.directoryFactory=HdfsDirectoryFactory -Dsolr.lock.type=hdfs -Dsolr.data.dir=hdfs://<host>:19000/solr -Dsolr.updatelog=hdfs:// <host>:19000/Solr-logs -jar start.jar
   ```

   You can validate the Solr on HDFS by accessing the Solr admin UI, to see it running on HDFS as shown in following screenshot:

   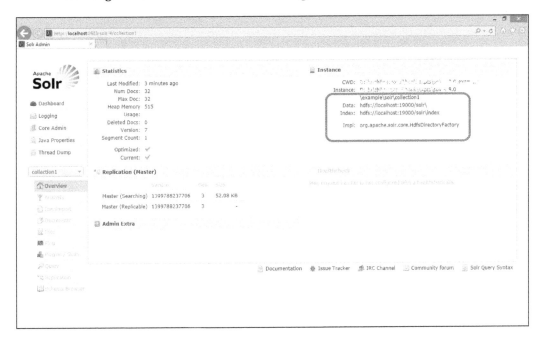

7. In case you are using Apache SolrCloud, you can point `solr.hdfs.home` to your HDFS folder, and keep the data and logs on the local machine.

   ```
   java -Dsolr.directoryFactory=HdfsDirectoryFactory -Dsolr.lock.type=hdfs -Dsolr.hdfs.home=hdfs://<host>:19000/solrhdfs -jar start.jar
   ```

Big data search using Katta

Katta provides highly scalable, fault-tolerant information storage. It is an open source project and uses the underlying Hadoop infrastructure (to be specific, HDFS) for storing its indices and providing access to them. Katta has been in the market for the last few years and while recently, the development on Katta has been stalled, there are still many users who go with Solr-Katta-based integration for big data search. Some organizations customize Katta as per their needs and utilize its capabilities for highly scalable search. Katta brings Apache Hadoop and Solr together, bringing search across a completely distributed MapReduce-based cluster. You can read more information about Katta on `http://katta.sourceforge.net/`.

How Katta works?

Katta can be primarily used with two different functions. The first is generating the Solr index, and the second is by running a search on the Hadoop cluster. The following diagram depicts what the Katta architecture looks like:

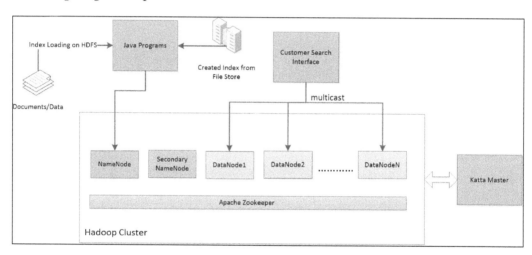

The Katta cluster has a master node called Katta Master. All other nodes are participants and are responsible for storing the data in their own local store by using HDFS or any other file system (if Katta is not used with Hadoop). Katta concepts are similar to Hadoop; each index is divided into multiple shards, and these shards are stored on the participating nodes. Each node also contains a content server to determine which type of shard is supported by a given Katta participating node.

Katta Master is responsible for communicating with nodes. Apache ZooKeeper communicates between Katta Master and the other participating nodes. All the nodes share a common folder (virtual folder) as supported by Apache ZooKeeper. This is where all the participating nodes keep the updated status of each node. This way, the Katta cluster does not require heartbeats, which are typically used by ZooKeeper clients for keeping the status of each node. The Katta cluster provides a blocking queue through which the overall work is divided among the nodes. Each node holds one queue, and the work is pushed to this queue. The node, after completing a task, looks at its queue for the next assignments one by one. The operations, such as shard deployment are supported by these queues.

Katta uses the multicasting concept for a search. The multicasting scope is determined by Katta Master based on the placement of shards, so when a search is requested, the client multicasts the query to the selected nodes through the use of the Hadoop Remote Procedure Calls (RPC) mechanism for faster direct communication. Each node then runs the query on its own shard and provides matching results with the scores. The scores are calculated across the Katta cluster node by node, so the merging of the result becomes easier. After merging them, ordering them as per the score, they are then returned to the client application.

Setting up the Katta cluster

Setting up the Katta cluster requires either downloading the distribution from `http://sourceforge.net/project/showfiles.php?group_id=225750` or building the source available on `http://katta.sourceforge.net/documentation/build-katta/`. If you are building the source, you need to run the following commands once you untar the source on Apache Ant version 1.6:

```
ant dist
```

The source will compile, and once it is completed, you will find the `distributed` folder created in the `$KATTA_ROOT/build` folder. You need to untar and copy `katta-core-VERSION.tar.gz` to all the participating nodes as well as master. Once copied, validate the deploy policy in the `katta.master.properties` file. Similarly, update the `katta.zk.properties` file as per your ZooKeeper configuration (ensemble or embedded). For embedded ZooKeeper, you need to modify the `zookeeper.servers` attribute for all nodes. You need to point to the master node. Now, you can start the master by running the following command:

```
bin/katta startMaster
```

[87]

Big Data Search Using Hadoop and Its Ecosystem

This will start the master at first. You should start the individual nodes on all machines by using the following command:

```
bin/katta startNode
```

Once all the nodes are started, you can start adding indexes to Katta.

Creating Katta indexes

Using Katta, you can either create a Hadoop map file-based index or use the Lucene index. You can also create your own type of shard. The Lucene index can be loaded on HDFS by importing the index in the Hadoop cluster. This is applicable to the exiting or already generated indexes.

You can alternatively use Hadoop's MapReduce capabilities to create an index out of normal documents. This is feasible by first transforming your data into the Hadoop sequential format with the help of the `net.sf.katta.indexing.SequenceFileCreator` class. You can also use Katta's sample creator script (`http://katta.sourceforge.net/documentation/how-to-create-a-katta-index`). Please note that Katta runs on older versions of Hadoop (0.20). Once the index is created, you can deploy them by using the `addIndex` call as shown here:

```
bin/katta addIndex <index-name> hdfs://<location-of-index>
```

Once the index is created, you can validate the availability of the index by running a search with the following command:

```
bin/katta search <index-name> <field:search-string>
```

Katta also provides a web-based interface for monitoring and administration purposes. It can be started by running:

```
bin/katta startGui
```

It provides masters, node information, shards, and indexes on the administration UI. This application is developed using the Grails technology.

Although Katta provides a completely Hadoop-based distributed search, it lacks the speed, and users frequently have to customize the Katta code as per their requirements. Katta provides an excellent failover for the master and the slaves nodes that are replicated, making it eligible for an enterprise-level big data search. However, the search cannot be used in real time, due to limits on speed. Katta is also not actively developed by the developers. The Apache Solr development community initially tried to incorporate Katta in Solr, but due to the focus on and advancements in SolrCloud, it was not merged in Apache Solr. Apache Solr created a JIRA for integrating Katta in Solr (Please refer to `https://issues.apache.org/jira/browse/SOLR-1395`).

Using Solr 1045 Patch – map-side indexing

Apache Solr 1045 patch provides Solr users a way to build Solr indexes using the MapReduce framework of Apache Hadoop. Once created, this index can be pushed to Solr storage. The following diagram depicts the Mapper and Reducer in Hadoop:

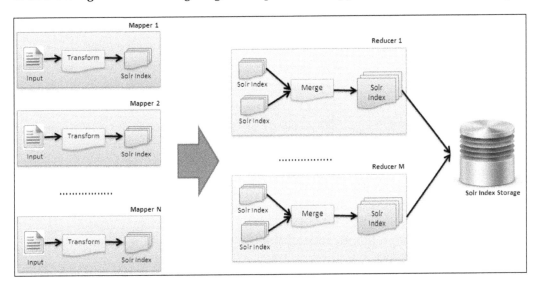

Each Apache Hadoop mapper transforms the input records into a set of (key, value) pairs, which then get transformed into SolrInputDocument. The Mapper task then ends up creating an index from SolrInputDocument.

The focus of Reducer is to perform de-duplication of different indexes and merge them if needed. Once the indexes are created, you can load them on your Solr instance and use them for searching. You can read more about this patch at https://issues.apache.org/jira/browse/SOLR-1045.

The patch follows the standard process of patching up your label through svn (Subversion). To apply a patch to your Solr instance, first, you need to build your Solr instance using source. The instance should be supported by Solr-1045 patch. Now, download the patch from Apache JIRA site (https://issues.apache.org/jira/secure/attachment/12401278/SOLR-1045.0.patch). Before running the patch, first do a dry run, which does not actually apply a patch. You can do it with the following command:

```
cd <Solr-trunk-dir>
svn patch <name-of-patch> --dry-run
```

Big Data Search Using Hadoop and Its Ecosystem

If the dry run works without any failure, you can apply the patch directly. You can also perform the dry run by using a simple patch command:

```
patch <name-of-patch> --dry-run
```

Once it is successful you can run the patch without the `-dry-run` option to apply the patch. On Windows, you can apply the patch with the right click:

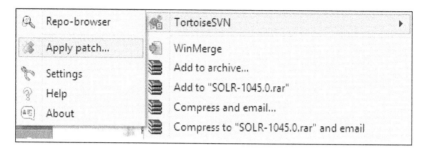

On Linux, you can use svn path as shown in the previous example. Let's look at some of the important classes in the patch. The `SolrIndexUpdateMapper` class is responsible for creating new indexes from the input document. The `SolrXMLDocRecordReader` class reads Solr input XML files for indexing. The `SolrIndexUpdater` class is responsible for creating a MapReduce job and running it to read the document and updating the Solr instance.

>
> Although Apache Solr patch 1045 provides an excellent parallel mapper and reducer, when the indexing is done at the map side, all the <key, value> pairs received by the reducer gain equal weight/importance. So, it is difficult to use this patch with data that carries ranking/weight information.

This patch also provides a way for users to merge the indexes in the reducer phase of the patch. This patch is not yet part of the Solr label, but it is targeted for the Solr 4.9/5.0 label.

Using Solr 1301 Patch – reduce-side indexing

The Solr 1301 patch is responsible for generating an index using the Apache Hadoop MapReduce framework. This patch is merged in Solr version 4.7 and is available in the code-line if you take Apache Solr with 4.7+ versions. This patch is similar to the previously discussed patch (SOLR-1045), but the difference is that the indexes that are generated using Solr 1301 are in the reduce phase and not in the map phase of Apache Hadoop's MapReduce. Once the indexes are generated, they can be loaded on Solr or SolrCloud for further processing and application searching. The following diagram depicts the overall flow:

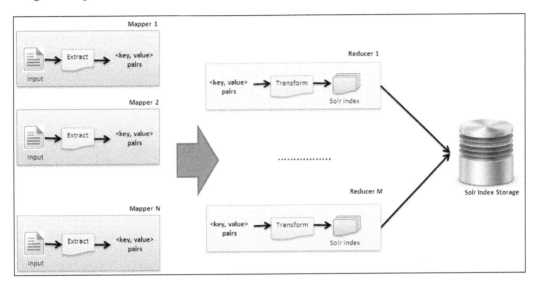

In case of Solr 1301, a map task is responsible for converting input records into a <key, value> pair. Later, they are passed to the reducer. The reducer is responsible for converting and publishing SolrInputDocument, which is then transformed into Solr indexes. The indexes are then persisted on HDFS directly and can later be exported to a Solr instance. In the latest Solr instance, this patch is part of the contrib module in the $SOLR_HOME\contrib\map-reduce folder. The patch/contrib map-reduce folder provides a MapReduce job that allows a user to build Solr indexes and merge them in the Solr cluster optionally.

Big Data Search Using Hadoop and Its Ecosystem

You will require a Hadoop cluster to run a solr 1301 patch. The solr 1301 patch is merged in Solr version 4.7 and is part of Solr contrib already. Once Hadoop is set, you can run the following command:

```
$HADOOP_HOME/bin/hadoop --config $HADOOP_CONF_DIR jar $SOLR_HOME/
contrib/dist/solr-map-reduce-*.jar -D 'mapred.child.java.opts=-Xmx500m'
--morphline-file readAvroContainer.conf --zk-host 127.0.0.1:9983
--output-dir hdfs://127.0.0.1:8020/outdir --collection collection1
--log4j log4j.properties --go-live --verbose "hdfs://127.0.0.1:8020/
indir"
```

In this command, the `config` parameter requires the configuration folder path of the Hadoop setup, the `mapred.child.java.opts` parameter passes the parameters to MapReduce programs, while the `zk-host` parameter points to an Apache ZooKeeper instance, the output-dir is where the output of this program should be stored, `collection` points to the collection in Apache Solr, log4j provides pointers to the log, the `go-live` option enables the merging of the output shards of the previous phase into a set of live customer-facing Solr servers, and `morphline-file` provides the configuration of the Avro-based pipe.

This will run the mapper and the reducer to generate a Solr index. Once the index is created through a Hadoop patch, it will be provisioned to the Solr server. The patch contains the default converter for CSV files. Let's look at some of the important classes that are a part of this patch. The `CSVDocumentConverter` class takes care of converting the output of `mapper(key,value)` to `SolrInputDocument`. The `CSVReducer` class provides the reducer implementation of the Hadoop Reduce cluster. The `CSVIndexer` class has to be called from the command line to run or create indexes using MapReduce; similarly, the `CSVMapper` class provides an introspection of the CSV and finally extracts with the key-value pairs. It requires additional parameters such as paths to point and output for storing shards. The `SolrDocumentConverter` class is responsible for transforming custom objects into SolrInputDocument. This class transforms (key, value) pairs into data that resides in HDFS or locally. The `SolrRecordWriter` class provides an extension over the MapReduce record writer. It divides the data into multiple pairs; these pairs are then transformed into the `SolrInputDocument` form.

Follow these steps to run this patch:

1. Create a local folder with the configuration and the `lib` folder, a conf file containing the Solr configuration (`solr-config.xml`, `schema.xml`), and lib folder, which contains the library.

[92]

2. `SolrDocumentConverter` provides an abstract class for writing your own converters. Create your own converter class implementing `SolrDocumentConverter`; this will be used by `SolrOutputFormat` to convert output records to Solr document. If required, override the `OutputFormat` class provided in Solr by your own extension.

3. Write a simple Hadoop MapReduce job in the configuration writer:

```
SolrOutputFormat.setupSolrHomeCache(new File(solrConfigDir),
conf);
conf.setOutputFormat(SolrOutputFormat.class);
SolrDocumentConverter.setSolrDocumentConverter(<your classname>.
class, conf);
```

4. Zip your configuration, and load it in HDFS. The zip file name should be `solr.zip` (unless you change the patch code).

5. Now, run the patch; each job will instantiate `EmbeddedSolrInstance`, which will in turn do the conversion, and finally, `SolrOutputDocument` will be stored in the output format.

With reduce-sized index generation, it is possible preserve the weights of documents, which can contribute to the prioritization performed during a search query.

Merging of indexes is not possible as in Solr 1045 because the indexes are created in the reduce phase. The reducer becomes the crucial component of the system as the major tasks are performed in the reducer.

Distributed search using Apache Blur

Apache Blur is a distributed search engine that can work with Apache Hadoop. It is different from the traditional big data system in that it provides a relational data model-like storage, on top of HDFS. Apache Blur does not use Apache Solr; however, it consumes Apache Lucene APIs. Blur provides faster data ingestion using MapReduce and advanced searches such as a faceted search, fuzzy, pagination, and a wildcard search.

Apache Blur provides a row-based data model (similar to RDBMS), with unique row IDs. Records should have a unique record ID, row ID, and column family. Column family is a group of logical columns. For example, the personal information column family will have columns such as name, companies with which the person works, and contact information. The following figure shows how Apache Blur works closely with Apache Hadoop:

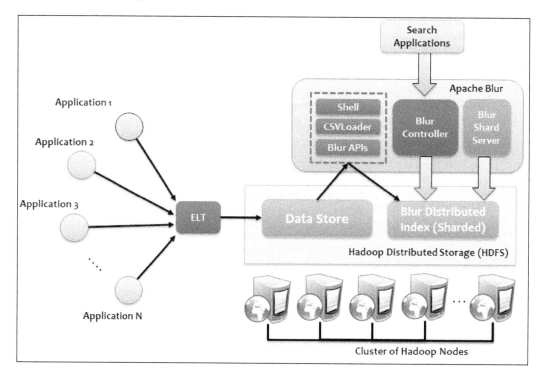

Apache Blur uses Hadoop to store its indexes in a distributed manner. It uses Thrift APIs for all interprocess communication. Blur Shard Server is responsible for managing shards, their availability, and so on, by using Apache ZooKeeper. Blur Controller provides a single point of access to the Apache Blur cluster.

Setting up Apache Blur with Hadoop

The current version of Apache Blur (0.2.3) works with Hadoop 1.x and 2.x. However, 2.x is not yet validated for scalability. We will set up Apache Blur with Apache Hadoop 1.2.1, load Hadoop with data, index it using Apache Blur, and search for it:

1. Apache Blur can be downloaded directly from the site http://incubator.apache.org/blur/. Download Hadoop1 Binary.

Chapter 4

2. Unzip the binary in your user folder with the following command:

```
hrishi@nova:~$ tar -xvzf apache-blur-<version>-hadoop1-bin.tar.gz
```

3. Now, download Apache Hadoop 1.2.1 from the following site: http://www.apache.org/dyn/closer.cgi/hadoop/common/.

4. Now, set up the Hadoop single node or a cluster with the help of Apache Documentation (link: https://hadoop.apache.org/docs/r1.2.1/#Getting+Started) (you will also find the Hadoop 1.X setup in the previous version of this book).

5. Once Apache Hadoop is set up, you can start the Hadoop cluster with the start-all.sh command.

6. Start Blur from the command line as shown in the following screenshot:

```
hrishi@nova:~/apache-blur-0.2.3-incubating-hadoop1-bin$ ./bin/start-all.sh
localhost: ZooKeeper starting as process 9098.
localhost: Shard [0] starting as process 9190.
localhost: Controller [0] starting as process 9282.
hrishi@nova:~/apache-blur-0.2.3-incubating-hadoop1-bin$
```

7. Take the CSV file (education-info.csv) provided in the blur folder of this book, and load it in Hadoop DFS with the following command. This CSV file contains sample data with pre-seeded row IDs and record IDs. In case you do not have these, you can provide -A (to generate row IDs), and -a (to generate record IDs):

```
hrishi@nova:~/hadoop $ ./bin/hadoop dfs -copyFromLocal blur/
education-info.csv hdfs://<ip-address>:<port>/education/sample
```

8. We are going to index this file in Apache Blur, but first, we need to create a table. This can be done in various ways. We will do it through the blur shell:

```
hrishi@nova: ~/apache-blur-0.2.3-incubating-hadoop1-bin
hrishi@nova:~/apache-blur-0.2.3-incubating-hadoop1-bin$ ./bin/blur shell
blur (default)> create -t educationinfo -c 1 -l hdfs://localhost:9000/educationinfo
blur (default)> list
enabled        -        educationinfo
blur (default)>
```

In this case, -c indicates the number of shards to be created. You will find the details of all shell commands at https://incubator.apache.org/blur/docs/0.2.3/using-blur.html#shell_table_commands.

[95]

Big Data Search Using Hadoop and Its Ecosystem

9. Now, create the indexes in Blur by using the CSV loader, the following screenshot shows how you can load it in blur:

```
hrishi@nova:~/blur $ ./bin/blur csvloader -t educationinfo -c
localhost:40010 -I localhost:9000/education/sample -d education
degree school year -d presonalinfo personname company phone
```

```
hrishi@nova:~/apache-blur-0.2.3-incubating-hadoop1-bin$ ./bin/blur csvloader -t educationinfo -c localhost:40010 -i
host:9000/education/sample -d education degree school year -d personalinfo personname. company. phone
Warning: $HADOOP_HOME is deprecated.

WARN  LoadSnappy - Snappy native library not loaded
hrishi@nova:~/apache-blur-0.2.3-incubating-hadoop1-bin$
```

10. Once your table is populated, you can simply run a query on blur to check the matching:

```
Blur (default)> query educationinfo personalinfo.
personname:Hrishikesh
```

```
1 results found in [741.926197 ms].  Row [1] Record [3] Column [9] Data (bytes) [334]
result# rowid recordid
0       1
                       education.degree        education.school        education.year
0               id1    Graduation              ABC Engineering         2009
0               id2    Diploma in Electronics  CDE College             2004
                       personalinfo.company    personalinfo.personname personalinfo.phone
0               id3    The Digital Group       Hrishikesh Karambelkar  58889833
```

Apache Solr and Cassandra

Cassandra is one of the most widely used distributed, fault-tolerant NoSQL databases. Cassandra is designed to handle big data workloads across multiple nodes with no single point of failure. There are some interesting performance benchmarks published at Planet Cassandra (`http://planetcassandra.org/NoSQL-performance-benchmarks/`), which places Apache Cassandra as one of the fastest NoSQL databases among its competitors in terms of the throughput, load, and so on. Apache Cassandra allows the schema-ess storage of user information in its store called the Column Families pattern. For example, look at the data model for sales lead information as shown in the following screenshot:

Customer Id	Name	Address	Contact Number	Designation	Revenue	Domain	Company Name
222	John C	1234, ABC Main, CA	9983988973				
123	David Alba		123434559		155 Billion		MyHome Corporation
432	Sunder Vishwanathan	6676, Park Avenue, IL				Energy Sector	
687			23444566	Architect			

[96]

This model, when transformed for the Cassandra store, becomes columnar storage. The following screenshot shows how this model would look using Apache Cassandra:

Customer ID			

222	Name	Address	Contact Number
	John C	1234, ABC Main, CA	9983988973

123	Name	Contact Number	Revenue	Company Name
	David Alba	123434559	155 Billion	MyHome Corporation

432	Name	Address	Domain
	Sunder Vishwanathan	6676, Park Avenue, IL	Energy Sector

687	Designation	Contact Number
	Architect	23444566

As one can see, the key here is the customer ID, and the value is a set of attributes/columns that vary for each row key. Further, columns can be compressed in order to reduce the size of your data footprint. The column compression is highly useful when you have common columns with repetitive values (for example, year or color). Cassandra partitions its data by using multiple strategies. All the nodes participating in the Cassandra cluster form a ring of nodes called the Cassandra ring. Column family data is partitioned across the nodes on the basis of the row key. To determine the node where the first replica of a row will live, the ring is walked clockwise until it locates the node with a token value greater than that of the row key. The data is partitioned on the basis of the hashing or ordered partitions, and is distributed across a cluster of nodes.

With heavy data, users cannot live with a single Solr node-based approach, and they move to a cluster approach. While Apache Solr provides an in-built SolrCloud, which seems to be capable of dealing with a huge dataset, many organizations still consider other options. This is because big data processing has multiple objectives beyond a pure search and querying. It is used for data analysis and predictions. Apache SolrCloud provides highly optimized index storage, particularly for search, and it cannot easily be used for any other purpose. Apache Cassandra is an open store that supports Hadoop-based MapReduce programs to be run on its datasets, and it can easily be integrated with any standard application. In cases where there are data usages beyond search and basic analysis, Apache Cassandra can serve as a single data store for multiple applications. Another reason for going ahead with the Cassandra-Solr combination is that Cassandra is a scalable and high-performance database.

Big Data Search Using Hadoop and Its Ecosystem

Working with Cassandra and Solr

There are two major approaches for integrating Cassandra with Solr. The first one is based on an open source application called Solandra, and the second one is based on DataStax Enterprise (DSE) Search built using Cassandra and Solr. There are differences between these two approaches in terms of integration with Solr. Solandra uses Cassandra instead of flat file storage for storing indexes in the lucene index format; DSE allows users to keep their data in Apache Cassandra and generate indexes using Cassandra's secondary index API, thus enabling other applications to consume the data for big data processing.

Solandra on the other hand uses legacy distributed search support from Apache Solr and allows the use of standard Apache Solr-based APIs, by hiding the underlying Cassandra-based distributed data storage. All the queries are fired through Apache Solr distributed search support and Cassandra, instead of flat files. Similarly, the indexing goes through the same overridden APIs.

We will be looking at the open source approach primarily. For integration using DSE, please visit: `http://www.datastax.com/download`.

Single node configuration

Solandra comes with in-built Solr and Cassandra, which can be used for development/evaluation purposes. It also has a sample dataset that can be loaded into Cassandra for initial testing. Although the active development of Solandra was stopped almost two years ago, it can still be used, and it can be extended to work with the latest Apache Solr instance. Let's go through the steps.

1. Download Solandra from `https://github.com/tjake/Solandra`.

2. Unzip the zip file. You will require Java as well as ant build scripting. You can download and unzip ant from `https://ant.apache.org/bindownload.cgi`.

3. Place the path of the `$ANT_HOME/bin` folder in your shell paths so that you would be able to run ant directly from the command line anywhere. Try running it from any folder, and you will see something like this:

```
$ ant -v
Apache Ant version 1.7.1 compiled on June 27 2008
Buildfile: build.xml does not exist!
Build failed
```

4. You will also require Apache Ivy to resolve Ivy dependency. You can download Ivy from `https://ant.apache.org/ivy/` and put it in the PATH.

[98]

Chapter 4

5. Now, go to `$SOLANDRA_HOME/solandra-app/conf` and open the cassandra. yaml file as shown in the following screenshot. Modify the paths to point to your temporary folder. In case of windows, it will be the `DRIVE:\tmp\ cassandra-data` folder. DRIVE is the name of the drive your Solandra is installed on. The `Cassandra.yaml` file is responsible for storing information on a cluster of nodes. As you can see, it uses a random partitioning algorithm, which applies hashing to each data element and places it in an appropriate node in a Cassandra cluster.

```
49  # - ByteOrderedPartitioner orders rows lexically by key bytes.  BOP allows
50  #    scanning rows in key order, but the ordering can generate hot spots
51  #    for sequential insertion workloads.
52  # - OrderPreservingPartitioner is an obsolete form of BOP, that stores
53  # - keys in a less-efficient format and only works with keys that are
54  #    UTF8-encoded Strings.
55  # - CollatingOPP colates according to EN,US rules rather than lexical byte
56  #    ordering.  Use this as an example if you need custom collation.
57  #
58  # See http://wiki.apache.org/cassandra/Operations for more on
59  # partitioners and token selection.
60  partitioner: lucandra.dht.RandomPartitioner
61
62  # directories where Cassandra should store data on disk.
63  data_file_directories:
64      - /tmp/cassandra-data/data
65
66  # commit log
67  commitlog_directory: /tmp/cassandra-data/commitlog
68
69  # Maximum size of the key cache in memory.
70  #
71  # Each key cache hit saves 1 seek and each row cache hit saves 2 seeks at the
72  # minimum, sometimes more. The key cache is fairly tiny for the amount of
73  # time it saves, so it's worthwhile to use it at large numbers.
```

Now, run ant from `$SOLANDRA_HOME`; this will create additional folders.

6. Once ant is complete, go inside Solandra-app and run

   $ bin/solandra

   This will start your server with Apache Solr and Cassandra together on one JVM.

7. You can load sample data for Reuters by going to `$SOLANDRA_HOME/reuter-demo`.

8. Download the sample dataset by calling:

   $ 1-download-data.sh

[99]

9. Load it in Solandra (Solr) by calling:

```
$ 2-import-data.sh
```

This script first loads Reuter's schema by using curl to `http://localhost:8983/solandra/schema/reuters` followed by data loading through Solandra's data loader (`reutersimporter.jar`).

Once this is done, you can run a select query on the router by calling `http://localhost:8983/solandra/reuters/select?q=*:*` from your browser to see the data coming from an embedded Solr-Cassandra-based single node Solandra instance. Along a similar line, you can also load your own schema on Solandra and use the data importer to import the data onto the Apache Solr instance. You can access the Solr configuration from the `$SOLANDRA_HOME/solandra-app/conf` folder.

The current Solandra version available for download uses Apache Solr 3.4, and it can be upgraded by modifying the library files of your Solr instance in `$SOLANDRA_HOME/solandra-app/lib` along with the configuration. In this configuration, Solandra uses its own index reader called SolandraIndexReaderFactory by overriding the default index reader as well as a search component (SolandraQueryComponent).

Integrating with multinode Cassandra

To work with the fully-working Apache Cassandra, you will need to perform the following steps:

1. First download Apache Cassandra from `http://cassandra.apache.org/`. If you already have Cassandra running, you can skip the following steps.

2. Unzip Cassandra and copy the library files of Solandra in solandra-app/lib to Cassandra's library folder (`$CASSANDRA_HOME/lib`), /bin folder to `$CASSANDRA_HOME/bin`, and the Solr configuration core files to the `$CASSANDRA_HOME/conf` folder. You can also run the following ant task:

```
ant -Dcassandra={unzipped dir} cassandra-dist
```

3. You can now start Solr within Cassandra by using the `$CASSANDRA_HOME/bin/solandra` command. Cassandra now takes two optional properties: `-Dsolandra.context` and `-Dsolandra.port` for the context path and the Jetty port. With the latest Cassandra version, you may get the incompatible class exception and may have to compile the solandra source against newer libraries or go back to the older Cassandra version (Version 1.1).

Scaling Solr through Storm

Apache Storm is a real time distributed computation framework. It processes humongous data in real time. Recently, Storm has been adapted by Apache as the incubating project and the development for Apache Storm. You can read more information about Apache Storm Features here: `http://storm.incubator.apache.org/`.

Apache Storm can be used to process massive streams of data in a distributed manner. It therefore provides excellent batch-oriented processing capabilities for time-sensitive analytics. With Apache Solr and Storm together, organizations can process big data in real time: for example, such industrial plants that would like to extract information from their plant system, which is emitting raw data continuously, and process it to facilitate real-time analytics such as identifying the top problematic systems or looking for recent errors/failures. Apache Solr and Storm can work together to execute such batch processing for big data in real time.

Apache Storm runs in a cluster mode where multiple nodes participate in performing computation in real time. It supports two types of nodes: a master node (also called Nimbus) and a worker node (also called a **slave**). As the name describes, Nimbus is responsible for distributing code around the cluster, assigning tasks to machines, and monitoring for failures, whereas the supervisor listens for work assigned to its machine and starts and stops worker processes as necessary on the basis of what Nimbus has assigned to it. Apache Storm uses ZooKeeper to perform all the co-ordination between Nimbus and the supervisor. The data in Apache Storm is ready as a stream, which is simply a tuple of name value pairs:

```
{id: 1748, author_name: "hrishi", full_name: "Hrishikesh Karambelkar"}
```

Apache Storm uses the concept of Spout and Bolts. All work is executed in the Apache Storm topology. The following screenshot shows the Storm topology with an example of word count:

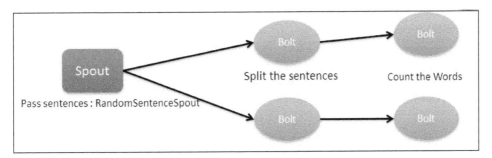

Big Data Search Using Hadoop and Its Ecosystem

Spouts are data inputs; this is where data arrives in the Storm cluster. Bolts process the streams that get piped into it. They can be fed data from spouts or other bolts. The bolts can form a chain of processing, with each bolt performing a unit task. This concept is similar to MapReduce, which we will discuss in the following chapters.

Getting along with Apache Storm

Let's install Apache Storm and try out a simple word count example:

1. You will require ZooKeeper to be downloaded first since both Nimbus and the supervisor have dependencies on them. You can download it from `http://zookeeper.apache.org/` and unzip it at some place. Copy `zoo.cfg` from the book's codebase, or rename `zoo_sample.cfg` to `zoo.cfg` in your code.

2. Start the ZooKeeper:

   ```
   $ bin/zkServer.sh
   ```

3. Make sure ZooKeeper is running. Now, download Apache Storm from `http://storm.incubator.apache.org/downloads.html`.

4. Unzip it, and go to the `$STORM_HOME/conf` folder. Edit storm.yaml and put the correct Nimbus host. You can use the configuration file provided along with the book. If you are running it in a cluster environment, your nimbus_host needs to point to the correct master. In this configuration, you may also provide multiple ZooKeeper servers for failsafe.

5. Now, set `JAVA_HOME` and `STORM_HOME`:

   ```
   $ export STORM_HOME=/home/hrishi/storm
   $ export JAVA_HOME=/usr/share/jdk
   ```

6. Start the master in a separate terminal by running:

   ```
   $ $STORM_HOME/bin/storm nimbus
   ```

7. Start workers on machines by calling:

   ```
   $ $STORM_HOME/bin/storm supervisor
   ```

8. Start the web interface by running:

   ```
   $ $STORM_HOME/bin/storm ui
   ```

Chapter 4

9. Now, access the web user interface by typing `http://localhost:8080` from your browser. A screen similar to the following screenshot should be visible now:

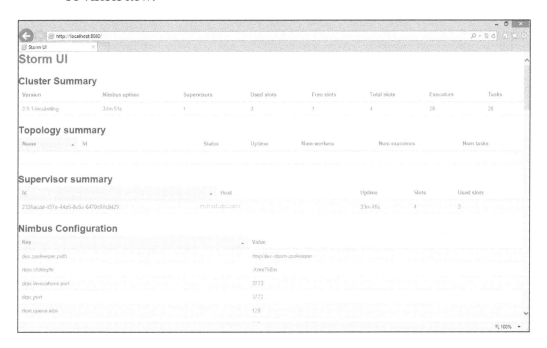

10. Now that the Storm cluster is working fine, let's try a simple word count example from `https://github.com/nathanmarz/storm-starter`. You can download the source and compile, or take a pre-compiled jar from the book source code repository.

11. You also need to install python on your instances where Apache Storm is running, in order to run this example. You can download and install python from `https://www.python.org/`. Once python is installed and added in the PATH environment, you can run the following command to start the word count task:

```
$ bin/storm jar storm-starter-0.0.1-SNAPSHOT-jar-with-dependencies.jar storm.starter.WordCountTopology WordCount -c nimbus.host=<host>
```

[103]

In the word count example, you will find different classes being mapped to different roles as shown in the following code snippet:

```
                                                    WordCountTopology.java
public static void main(String[] args) throws Exception {

  TopologyBuilder builder = new TopologyBuilder();

  builder.setSpout("spout", new RandomSentenceSpout(), 5);

  builder.setBolt("split", new SplitSentence(), 8).shuffleGrouping("spout");
  builder.setBolt("count", new WordCount(), 12).fieldsGrouping("split", new Fields("word"));

  Config conf = new Config();
  conf.setDebug(true);


  if (args != null && args.length > 0) {
    conf.setNumWorkers(3);

    StormSubmitter.submitTopology(args[0], conf, builder.createTopology());
  }
  else {
```

Advanced analytics with Solr

Apache Solr provides excellent searching capabilities on the metadata. It is also possible to go beyond a search and faceting with the help of the integration space. As the search industry grows into the next generation, the expectations that search will go beyond a basic search has led to the creation of software such as Apache Solr, which is capable of providing an excellent browsing and filtering experience. It provides basic analytical capabilities. However, for many organizations, this is not sufficient. They would like to bring in capabilities of business intelligence and analytics on top of search engines. Today, it is possible to complement Apache Solr with such advanced analytical capabilities. We will be looking at enabling Solr integration with R.

R is an open source language and environment for statistical computing and graphics. More information about R can be found at http://www.r-project. org/. The development of R started in 1994 as an alternative to SAS, SPSS, and other proprietary statistical environments. R is an integrated suite of software facilities for data manipulation, calculation, and graphic display. There are around 2 million R users worldwide, and it is widely taught in universities. Many corporate analysts know and use R. R provides hundreds of open source packages to enhance productivity, such as:

- Linear and non-linear modeling
- Classical statistical tests

- Time-series analysis
- Spatial statistics
- Classification, clustering, and other capabilities
- Matrix arithmetic, with scalar, vector, matrices, list, and data frame (aka table) structures
- Extensive library functions (more than 2000) for different graphs/charts

Integrating R with Solr provides organizations with access to these extensive library functions, so that they can perform data analysis on Solr outputs.

Integrating Solr and R

Since R is an analytical engine, it can work on top of Apache Solr to perform a direct analysis on the results of Apache Solr. R can be installed directly through executable installers (.exe/.rpm/bin) that can be downloaded from cran mirrors (http://cran.r-project.org/mirrors.html) for any *nix, Windows, or Mac OS. R can connect to Apache Solr through the CURL utility built in as the RCURL library in R packages. R also provides a library called Solr to use Solr capabilities to search over user data, extracted content, and so on. To enable R with Solr, open the R console from and run:

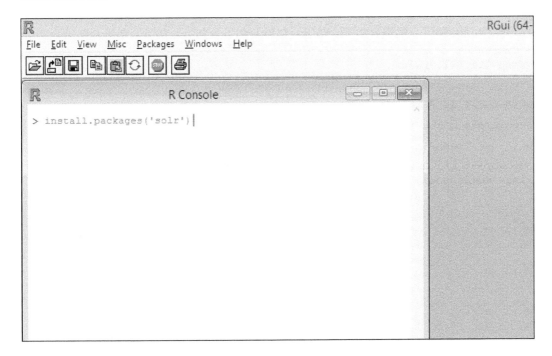

Big Data Search Using Hadoop and Its Ecosystem

Now, to test it, fire a search on your Solr server:

```
> library(solr)
```

To test analytics, let us take a simple use case. Assume that there is a multinational job recruitment firm and it is using Apache Solr built on top of candidate resumes. The expectation is to provide facets such as technical capabilities and country. Now, using Apache Solr, they would like to decide which countries to focus their business for certain technology (let's say Solr). So, they would like to classify the countries based on the current available resource pool for Apache Solr. R provides various clustering algorithms, which can provide users with different clusters of data based on characteristics. One of the most widely used algorithms is K-means clustering (More information can be read on http://en.wikipedia.org/wiki/K-means_clustering). To use K-means in R, and plot the graph, you will be required to install the package cluster by calling

```
> install.packages('cluster')
```

After the installation of the cluster package, get the facet information using the Solr package of R and process it for K-means. Run the following R script on the console to get the cluster information:

```
> library(cluster)
> library(solr)
> url <- 'http://localhost:8983/solr/select'
> response1 <- solr_group(q='*:Solr', group.field='Country', rows=10,
group.limit=1, base=url)
> m2 <- matrix(response1$numFound,byrow=TRUE)
> rownames(m2) <- response1$groupValue
> colnames(m2) <- 'Available Workforce';
> fit <- kmeans(m2, 2)
> clusplot(m2, fit$cluster, color=TRUE, shade=TRUE,labels=2, lines=0,
xlab="Workforce", ylab="Cluster", main="K-Means Cluster")
```

[106]

Once you run the `clusplot()` function, you should be able to get a graphical representation of the cluster as shown in the following screenshot:

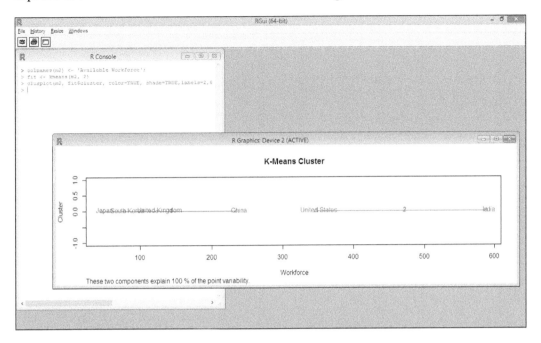

The cluster plot in this screenshot demonstrates how Apache Solr search analytics can be used for further advanced analytics using the R statistical language.

Summary

In this chapter, we have discussed different ways in which Apache Solr can be scaled to work with big data/large datasets. We looked at different implementations of Solr-big data such as Solr-HDFS, Katta, Solr-1045, Solr 1301, and Apache Solr with Cassandra. We also looked at advanced analytics by integrating Apache Solr with R. In the next chapter, we will focus on improving the performance for big data.

Scaling Search Performance

5

As the data grows, it impacts the time taken for both search, as well as creating new indexes to keep up with the increasing size of the repository. The simplest way to preserve the same search performance while scaling your data is to keep increasing your hardware, which includes higher processing power and higher memory size. However, this is not a cost-effective alternative. So, instead we will want to look for optimizing the running of the big data search instance. We have also covered different architectures of Solr in *Chapter 4*, *Big Data Search Using Hadoop and Its Ecosystem*, among which the most suitable architecture can be chosen on the basis of the requirements and the usage patterns.

The overall optimization of the technology stack, which includes Apache Hadoop and Apache Solr, helps you maintain more data with reasonable performance. The optimization is most important while scaling your instance for big data with Hadoop and Solr. We are going to look at different techniques of improving performances for your big data Search. Optimization can be done on different levels:

- Optimizing search schema
- Optimizing the indexes
- Optimizing the J2EE container
- Optimization search runtime
- Monitoring your setup for performance and impact

[109]

Scaling Search Performance

Understanding the limits

Although you can have a completely distributed system for your big data search, there is a limit in terms of how far you can go. As you keep on distributing the shards, you may end up facing what is called the "**laggard problem**" for indexes for your instance.

This problem states that the response to your search query, which is an aggregation of results from all the shards, is controlled by the following formula:

```
QueryResponse = avg(max(shardResponseTime))
```

This means that if you have many shards, it is more likely that you will have one of them responding slowly (due to some anomaly) to your queries, and this will impact on your query response time, and this will start increasing.

The distributed search in Apache Solr has many limitations. Each document uploaded as distributed big data must have a unique key, and this unique key must be stored in the Solr repository. To do so, the Solr `schema.xml` file should have "`stored=true`" against the key attribute. This unique key has to be unique across all shards. Some of the features such as More Like This, Join, and Query Elevation Component do not work in the Solr distributed environment.

When running Solr in a distributed manner, you may face the issue of **Distributed Deadlock**. When a query is passed to a shard, it can make sub-queries to all other shards. Now, once the work is assigned, and the shards are busy serving their own request that depends upon completing another's request, it would have an indefinite wait time for the search query. Let's say that there are two shards, and each of them got a job for processing. They create sub-tasks, which are then assigned to each other's threads. Both the requests are waiting for the other shard to complete the task. This is called **Distributed Deadlock**.

Apache Lucene does have a cap on the size of index (approximately limiting it to 2 billion documents in total). However, theoretically, there is no limit to the number of documents that can be loaded on big data search indexing while running in the distributed mode.

Optimizing search schema

When Solr is used in the context of a specific requirement (for example, log search for an enterprise application) it holds a specific schema that can be defined in `schema.xml` and copied over to nodes. The schema is based on the schema attributes indexes and thus plays a vital role in the performance of your Solr instance.

Specifying default search field

In the `schema.xml` file of the Solr configuration, the system allows you to specify the `<defaultSearchField>` parameter. This is the parameter that controls when you search without an explicit field name in your query, and which field to pick up for searching. This is an optional parameter; if this is not specified, for all the queries that are not providing the field name, the search will run them on all the available fields in the schema. This will not only consume more CPU time but on the whole, slow down the search performance.

Configuring search schema fields

In custom schema, having a larger number of fields for indexing has a direct impact on the index size and the amount of memory needed to create your index and segments. You can control the amount of indexing of fields to be done by specifying `indexed=true` or `indexed=false` appropriately for each schema attribute. Avoid indexing unnecessary fields that you do not intend to use in the search.

Similarly, you can set `stored=false` for fields that are not returned as search results. Setting this will not stop you from querying for these fields, but you won't be able to retrieve the original value of these fields. For larger fields, there is a significant value to this? in terms of disk space and search speed for the lookup.

The fields that are larger are difficult to fit into the memory while indexing, so one has to ensure that all the fields of the document fit into the memory. Each field can have `maxFieldLength` in the schema configuration; this in turn can help you control the sizing of the fields.

Scaling Search Performance

Stop words

We have already covered stop words in *Chapter 2, Understanding Apache Solr*, and *Appendix, Use Cases for Big Data Search*, which provides more details about them. They play a significant role in optimizing your Solr instance for performance. While performing the inverted index creation, the stop words are not considered by Solr because they do not add any value to your search. The stop words can be specified in any file and the file can be pointed out in the `schema.xml` file of the Solr configuration.

```
435    <!-- A general text field that has reasonable, generic
436         cross-language defaults: it tokenizes with StandardTokenizer,
437      removes stop words from case-insensitive "stopwords.txt"
438      (empty by default), and down cases.  At query time only, it
439      also applies synonyms. -->
440    <fieldType name="text_general" class="solr.TextField" positionIncrementGap="100">
441      <analyzer type="index">
442        <tokenizer class="solr.StandardTokenizerFactory"/>
443        <filter class="solr.StopFilterFactory" ignoreCase="true" words="stopwords.txt"
444        <!-- in this example, we will only use synonyms at query time
445        <filter class="solr.SynonymFilterFactory" synonyms="index_synonyms.txt" ignored
446        -->
447        <filter class="solr.LowerCaseFilterFactory"/>
448    </fieldType>
```

```
a
an
the
will
then
their
my
with
within
is
are
was
may
can
```

Having a large set of stop words can significantly save space in terms of index size creation. You can use some of the common stop words of the English language by accessing the following example links:

- `http://xpo6.com/list-of-english-stop-words/`

- `http://dev.mysql.com/doc/refman/5.5/en/fulltext-stopwords.html`

- `http://www.textfixer.com/resources/common-english-words.txt`

Stemming

Stemming is a process of reducing the derived word into its original form. By enabling word stemming with Apache Solr, it not only saves your search time but also improves your query performance. Stemming also improves the accuracy of the results. For example words such as `walking`, `walked`, and `walks` can be stemmed to `walk`. *Appendix, Use Cases for Big Data Search*, provides a detailed explanation about `protwords.txt`, which is used for stemming, along with some examples. Based on the requirements, a right stemming algorithm should be chosen for your instance. Here are some of the available algorithms for stemming:

Algorithm	Description
Porter	This rule-based algorithm transforms any form of the word in English into its stem. For example, talking and talked are marked as talk.
KStem	Similar to Porter, with less aggressiveness.

Chapter 5

Algorithm	Description
Snowball	This is all language-supported string processing language for running your words. Using this, you can create new stemming algorithms.
Hunspell	Open Office dictionary-based algorithm. Works with all languages; the only condition is the health of the dictionary.

Overall, the workflow and the mandatory fields for mapping are shown in the following table. A true value indicates the presence of this attribute while defining the field, and a false value indicates that it cannot be used for a given use case. For example, a multi-valued attribute cannot be used in unique keys. An empty value indicates that the attribute can be true or false. We have already explained the terms multi-valued, omit-norms, term vector, and so on in *Chapter 2, Understanding Apache Solr*:

Use Case	Indexed	Stored	Multi-valued	Omit Norms	Term Vectors	Term Positions	Term Offsets
Search within field	TRUE						
Retrieve contents		TRUE					
Use as unique key	TRUE		FALSE				
Sort on field	TRUE		FALSE	TRUE			
Use field boosts				FALSE			
Document boosts affect searches within field				FALSE			
Highlighting	TRUE	TRUE					
Faceting	TRUE						
Add multiple values, maintaining order			TRUE				
Field length affects doc score				FALSE			
MoreLikeThis		TRUE			TRUE		
Term frequency					TRUE		

[113]

Use Case	Indexed	Stored	Multi-valued	Omit Norms	Term Vectors	Term Positions	Term Offsets
Document frequency					TRUE		
tf*idf					TRUE		
Term positions					TRUE	TRUE	TRUE
Term offsets					TRUE	TRUE	TRUE

Index optimization

The indexes used in Apache Solr are inverted indexes. In case of the inverted indexing technique, all your text will be parsed and words will be extracted out of it. These words are then stored as index items, with the location of their appearance. For example, consider the following statements:

1. "Mike enjoys playing on a beach"
2. "Playing on the ground is a good exercise"
3. "Mike loves to exercise daily"

The index with location information for all these sentences will look like following (Numbers in brackets denote (sentence number, word number)):

```
Mike      (1,1), (3,1)
enjoys    (1,2)
playing   (1,3), (2,1)
on        (1,4), (2,2)
a         (1,5), (2,5)
beach     (1,6)
ground    (2,3)
is        (2,4)
good      (2,6)
loves     (3,2)
to        (3,3)
exercise  (2,7), (3,4)
daily     (3,5)
```

When you perform a delete on your inverted index, it does not delete the document; it only marks the document as deleted. It will get cleaned only when the segment that the index is a part of is merged. When you create an index, you should avoid modifying the index.

Limiting indexing buffer size

As the index size grows, the Solr instance starts using up more CPU time and memory to perform a faceted search. When the indexes are first created, the overall operation runs in the batch mode. All the documents are kept in memory until it exceeds the RAM buffer size specified in `solr-config.xml`:

```
<ramBufferSizeMB>100</ramBufferSizeMB>
```

Once the size is exceeded, Solr creates a new segment or merges the index with the current segment. The default value of the RAM buffer size is 100 MB (Solr 1.4 onwards). Similarly, there is another parameter that controls the maximum number of documents in the buffer of Solr while indexing:

```
<maxBufferedDocs>1000</maxBufferedDocs>
```

When an indexed document crosses the limits defined for both the RAM buffer size and the maximum number of buffer documents, it will flush the changes. You can also control the maximum number of threads used for indexing the document by tuning `maxIndexingThread`; the default value is 8. By setting this parameter appropriately as per your usage, you can speed up your indexing process. By setting this parameter, you can use clients that can connect concurrently to the search server for uploading the data by using multiple threads. Solr provides the `ConcurrentUpdateSolrServer` class for the same.

The number of commit operations has to be decided optimally. Frequent commit operations eat more CPU/IO time, whereas few commit operations demand an increase in the memory size of your instance.

When to commit changes?

Commit is the operation that ensures that all the updates/uploads to Solr are stored on the disk. With Solr, you can perform commit in the following different ways:

- Automatic commit
- Soft commit

Scaling Search Performance

When autocommit is enabled, the document uploaded to Apache Solr gets written to the storage immediately. In case of a cluster environment, a hard commit will replicate the indexes across all the nodes. This condition is the maximum time (`maxTime`) or maximum number of documents (`maxDocs`) after which commit should take place. Choosing relatively low values for these works well for an environment where you have continuous index updates; this incurs a significant performance bottleneck for batch updates in a distributed environment. At the same time, having a high value for `maxTime` or `maxDocs` may pose a high risk of losing indexed documents in case of failures.

There is also an option called `openSearcher` in the handler definition of `solrconfig.xml`. When this value is set to true, it allows a new searcher to get initialized after the changes are committed to the storage. This option enables users to see the newly committed changes in their search results immediately. Each handler also has `updateLog`, which is a transaction log that enables the recovery of updates in case of failures; this therefore supports/enables durability.

> To achieve the maximum durability of a Solr instance, it is recommended to have a hard commit size limit based on the size of the update log.

Similar to hard commit is the soft commit. Soft commit is a faster alternative which, unlike hard commit, only makes the index changes visible for searches. It does not perform any sync of indexes across nodes. In case of a power failure of the machine, the changes made using soft commit are lost. With soft commit, Solr can achieve **near-real-time search** capabilities. You should have the soft commit maxTime set less than the hard commit time. Therefore, the configuration file would look as shown in the following screenshot:

```
<!-- The default high-performance update handler -->
<updateHandler class="solr.DirectUpdateHandler2">

    <updateLog>
        <str name="dir">${solr.ulog.dir:}</str>
    </updateLog>
    <autoCommit>
        <maxTime>15000</maxTime>
        <openSearcher>false</openSearcher>
    </autoCommit>

    <autoSoftCommit>
        <maxTime>1000</maxTime>
    </autoSoftCommit>
```

Solr also allows you to pass the commit request in your update request itself.

Chapter 5

Optimizing index merge

While creating index segments, the following flowchart depicts how Solr functions:

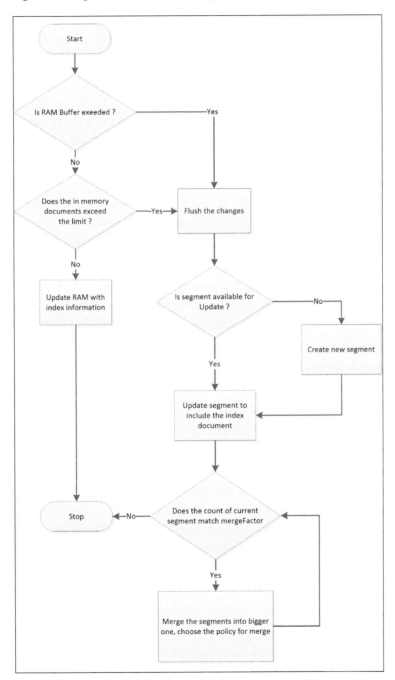

[117]

Scaling Search Performance

Solr keeps the newly updated index in the most recent segment; if the segment is filled up, it will create a new segment. Solr performs a merge of segments as and when the number of lowest-level segments is equal to `mergeFactor`, specified in the Solr configuration file. In such a case, it merges all the segments into one. Consider the following case:

```
<mergeFactor>20</mergeFactor>
```

The segments are merged when the number of lowest-level segments equals 20. This process continues. `mergeFactor` directly carries the impact on your search query time and indexing time. If you have a high mergeFactor, your index creation process will be faster as it does not really need to perform the merging of indexes; however, for a search, Solr has to look into multiple files in the file store. If you have a low mergeFactor, it will slow down your indexing process due to the need to perform a merge over huge indexes. The search will be relatively faster as it has to look at few files.

Optimize option for index merging

When this option is called, Solr runs the index merge operation, and it forces all the index segments to get merged into a single segment. This is an expensive operation, which in turn reads and rewrites all the indexes of Solr. It impacts the functioning of the search instance, so it is recommended to run this operation when there is no/less load on the instance. It provides additional attributes such as `waitFlush` (blocks the instance until the index changes are flushed to a disk), `waitSearcher` (blocks until a new searcher with all the changes visible is made available), and `maxSegment` (you can choose to optimize your instance to maximum segment listed here). Solr also allows you to call optimize through a URL call itself:

```
curl 'http://localhost:8983/solr/update?optimize=true&maxSegments=2&wa
itFlush=false'
```

While running in the SolrCloud environment, you should be careful while running optimize (forced merge) on your own, instead you can rely on Solr to perform optimization, as a partial merge (that which it does in background).

Optimizing the container

Most of the big data implementations including Solr and Hadoop run under J2EE container with some JDK. While scaling your instance for more data and more indexes, it becomes important to optimize your containers as well to ensure that you get optimal high-speed performance out of the system. Choosing the right JVM is therefore a very important factor. There are many JVMs available in the market today that can be considered, such as Oracle Java HotSpot, BEA JRockit, and Open Source JVM. You can look at comparisons between different JVMs at http://en.wikipedia. org/wiki/Comparison_of_Java_virtual_machines. Apache Solr allows you to run multiple Solr instances with their own JVMs. Zing JVM from the Azul system is considered to be a high-performance JVM for Solr/Lucene implementations.

Optimizing concurrent clients

You can control the number of concurrent connections that can be made in your container. This in turn reduces traffic on your instance, which may be running in a standalone/distributed environment.

In the tomcat server, you can simply modify the following entries in server.xml for changing the number of concurrent connections:

```
69      -->
70      <Connector port="10080" protocol="HTTP/1.1"
71              connectionTimeout="20000"
72              redirectPort="10443" acceptCount="100"/>
73      <!-- A "Connector" using the shared thread pool-->
```

Similarly, in Jetty, you can control the number of connections held by modifying jetty.xml:

```
48      <!-- This connector is currently being used for Solr because it
49          showed better performance than nio.SelectChannelConnector
50          for typical Solr requests.  -->
51      <Call name="addConnector">
52        <Arg>
53          <New class="org.eclipse.jetty.server.bio.SocketConnector">
54            <Set name="host"><SystemProperty name="jetty.host" /></Set>
55            <Set name="port"><SystemProperty name="jetty.port" default="8983"/></Set>
56            <Set name="maxIdleTime">50000</Set>
57            <Set name="lowResourceMaxIdleTime">1500</Set>
58            <Set name="Acceptors">20</Set>
59            <Set name="statsOn">false</Set>
60          </New>
61        </Arg>
62      </Call>
63
```

Optimizing Java virtual memory

One of the key optimization factors is controlling the virtual memory size of your big data Solr instance. This is applicable to instances running in the distributed environment, as well as the instances running as a standalone search instance. As your big data search instance scales with the data size, it requires more and more memory and it therefore becomes important to optimize accordingly. Apache Solr has an in-built cache, which should be one of the factors considered for optimization. Since both Hadoop and Solr run on JVMs, one has to look at the optimization of Java Virtual Machine (JVM).

All Solr instances run inside the J2EE container as applications, and all the common optimizations for applications are applicable to it. It starts with choosing the right heap size for your JVM. The heap size for JVM can be controlled by the following parameters.

Parameter	Description
-Xms	Minimum heap size required with which the container is initialized
-Xmx	Maximum heap size up to which the container is allowed to grow

When you choose the minimum heap size to be low, the initialization of the application itself might take more time. Similarly, having a higher minimum heap size may unnecessarily block the huge memory segment, which could be useful for your other processes. However, it will reduce the calls to resize the heap when the heap is full, since the heap holds more memory at the start time. Similarly, having a low maximum heap size may fail your application running in-between, throwing Out Of Memory exceptions for large indexes/objects of your search. When providing the memory size for JVM, you need to ensure that you keep sufficient memory for your operating system and other processes so as to avoid them going into the thrashing mode. In the production environment, it is better to keep the minimum and the maximum heap sizes the same, to avoid the overhead of the heap size.

> When you are running optimized Solr instances in the container, it is recommended not to install any other applications on the same container, so as to minimize the CPU time and the memory getting distributed among Solr and these applications.

Chapter 5

When the heap is full, JVM tries to grab more memory based on the –Xmx parameter. Before doing that, it performs **garbage collection**. Garbage collection in JVM is a process through which JVM reclaims the memory consumed by objects that are unused/expired/not referred by any of your application processes running in memory. Today's JVMs trigger the garbage collection process automatically as and when needed. The process can be explicitly called from the application code through the System.gc() call, and this will explicitly trigger the garbage collection process, cleaning up the garbage. Such explicit calls to garbage collection should be avoided for the following reasons:

- There is no control over whether the garbage collection process is run while your search/indexing is run.

- When the garbage collection process is run, it will end up taking your CPU time and memory, which impacts the overall functioning of the search.

- The heap size influences the time for running the garbage collection process. A longer heap size will make the garbage collector take more time to identify and clean the VM objects. New releases of Java (1.7 onwards) have some optimization over the garbage collection.

If you are using Solr faceting, or features like sorting, you will require more memory. The operating system performs memory swapping based on the needs of processors. This can create huge latency in any search with large indexes. Many of the operating systems allow users to control the swapping of programs.

Optimizing search runtime

The search runtime speed is also a primary concern, and so it should be performed. You can also perform optimization at various levels at runtime. When Solr fetches the results for the queries passed by the user, you can limit the fetching of the result to a certain number by specifying the rows attribute in your search. The following query will return 10 rows of results from 10 to 20.

```
q=Scaling Big Data&rows=10&start=10
```

This can also be specified in solrconfig.xml as queryResultWindowSize, thereby setting the size to a limited number of query results.

Let's look at various other optimizations possible in the search runtime.

[121]

Optimizing through search query

Whenever a query request is forwarded to a search instance, Solr can respond in various ways, such as XML or JSON. A typical Solr response not only contains information about the matched results, but also contains information about your facets, highlighted text, and many other things which are used by the client (by default, a velocity template-based client provided by Solr). This in turn is a heavy response and can be optimized by providing a compression over the result. Compressing the result, however, incurs more CPU time, and this may impact the response time and query performance. However, there is a significant value in terms of the response size that passes over the network.

Filter queries

A normal query on Solr will perform the search, and then apply a complex scoring mechanism to determine the relevance of the document that appeared with the search results. A filter query on Solr will perform the search and apply the filter; this does not apply any scoring mechanism. A query can easily be converted into a filter query:

```
Normally: q=name:Scaling Hadoop AND type:books
Filter Query: q=name:Scaling Hadoop&fq=type:books
```

The processing required for scoring is not needed; hence, it is faster than a normal query. Since the scoring is no more applicable with filter queries, if the same query is passed again and again, the results are returned from the filter cache directly.

Optimizing the Solr cache

Solr provides caching at various levels as a part of its optimization. For caching at these levels, there are multiple implementations available in Solr by default. `LRUCache` is the least recently used cache (based on synchronized `LinkedHashMap`), `FastLRUCache`, and `LFUCache` is the least frequently used cache (based on `ConcurrentHashMap`). Among these `FastLRUCache` is expected to be faster than all others. These caches are associated with search (index searchers).

> Cache Autowarming is a feature by which a cache can pre-populate itself with objects from old search instances/cache.

Chapter 5

These cache objects do not carry an expiry; they live as long as the index searches are alive. The configuration for different caches can be specified in `solrconfig.xml` as shown in the following screenshot:

```
433    <!-- ~~~~~~~~~~~~~~~~~~~~~~~~~~~~~~~~~~~~~~~~~~~~~~~~~~~~~~~~~~~~~~~~~
434        Query section - these settings control query time things like caches
435        ~~~~~~~~~~~~~~~~~~~~~~~~~~~~~~~~~~~~~~~~~~~~~~~~~~~~~~~~~~~~~~~~~ -->
436    <query>
437        <maxBooleanClauses>1024</maxBooleanClauses>
438        <filterCache class="solr.FastLRUCache"
439                     size="512"
440                     initialSize="512"
441                     autowarmCount="0"/>
442
443        <queryResultCache class="solr.LRUCache"
444                          size="512"
445                          initialSize="512"
446                          autowarmCount="0"/>
447        <documentCache class="solr.LRUCache"
448                       size="512"
449                       initialSize="512"
450                       autowarmCount="0"/>
451        <fieldValueCache class="solr.FastLRUCache"
452                         size="512"
453                         autowarmCount="128"
454                         showItems="32" />
455
```

There are common parameters to the cache:

Parameter	Description
Class	You can specify the type of cache you wish to attach, that is, LRUCache, FastLRUCache, or LFUCache.
Size	This is the maximum size a cache can reach.
initialSize	Initial size of the cache when it is initialized.
autowarmCount	The number of entries to seed from an old cache.
minSize	Applicable to FastLRUCache. After the cache reaches its peak size, it tries to reduce the cache size to minSize. The default value is 90 percent of the size.
acceptableSize	If FastLRUCache cannot reduce to minSize when the cache reaches its peak, it will at least reach acceptableSize.

All cache is initialized when a new index searcher instance is opened. Let's look at different caches in Solr and how you can utilize them for speeding up your search.

[123]

The filter cache

This cache is responsible for storing the documents for filter queries that are passed to Solr. Each filter is cached separately; when queries are filtered, this cache returns the results, and eventually, based on the filtering criteria, the system performs an intersection of them. If you have faceting, the use of a filter cache can improve performance. This cache stores the document IDs in an unordered state.

The query result cache

This cache will store the top N query results for each query passed by the user. It stores an ordered set of document IDs. For queries that are repeated, this cache is very effective. You can specify the maximum number of documents that can be cached by this cache in `solrconfig.xml`:

    <queryResultMaxDocsCached>200</queryResultMaxDocsCached>

The document cache

This cache primarily stores the documents that are fetched from the disk. Once a document loads into a cache, search does not then need to fetch it from the disk again, reducing your overall disk IOs. This cache works on the IDs of documents, so the autowarming feature does not really have any impact, since the document IDs keep changing as and when there is a change in index.

> The size of the document cache should be based on the size of the results and the size of the maximum number of queries allowed to run; this will ensure that there is no refetch of the document by Solr.

The field value cache

This cache is used mainly for faceting. If you have regularly use faceting, it makes sense to enable caching for field levels. This cache can also be used for sorting. It supports multivalued fields. You can monitor the caching status in the administration of Solr. It provides information such as current load, hit rations, and hits.

Chapter 5

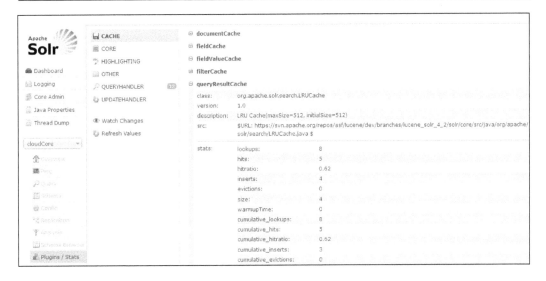

The lazy field loading

By default, Solr reads all stored fields and then filters the ones that are not needed. This becomes a performance overhead for a large number of fields. When this flag is set, only fields that are requested will be loaded immediately; the rest of the fields are loaded lazily. This offers significant improvement in the search speed. This can be done by setting the following flag in solconfig.xml:

```
<enableLazyFieldLoading>true</enableLazyFieldLoading>
```

In addition to these options, you can also define your cache implementation.

Optimizing Hadoop

When running Solr with Hadoop for indexing (Solr patches) or for search (Katta), the optimization of Hadoop adds performance benefits to a big data search instance. The optimization can be done at the storage level that is HDFS as well as at the level of the MapReduce programs. Hadoop should preferably run on 64-bit machines to allow administrators to go beyond the Java heap size of 3 GB (it is limited to 3 GB in 32 bit). You also need to set a high priority for Hadoop user jobs and scheduler.

Scaling Search Performance

While storing the indexes in a distributed environment like Hadoop, storing in a compressed format can improve the storage space as well as the memory footprint. This in turn reduces your disk IO and bytes transferred over wires, by adding an overhead for extracting it as and when needed. You can do that this by enabling `mapred.compress.map.output=true`. Another interesting parameter is the block size of a file for HDFS. This needs to be defined well; considering the fact that all indexes are stored in HDFS files, defining the appropriate block size (`dfs.block.size`) will be a great help. The number of MapReduce tasks can also be optimized based on the input size (the batch size of Solr documents for indexing/sharding). In case of Solr-1301, the output of reduce tasks are passed to `SolrOutputFormat`, which calls `SolrRecordWriter` for writing the data. After completing the reduce task, `SolrRecordWriter` calls `commit()` and `optimize()` for performing index merging. There are additional parameters that can definitely add value towards optimizations in `mapred-site.xml`:

Parameter	Description
`mapred.map.tasks.speculative.execution` / `mapred.reduce.tasks.speculative.execution`	Hadoop jobs can become slow for various reasons, such as other processes consuming memory or misconfiguration. The slowness is hard to detect. So, when such jobs take more time than expected, Hadoop launches a new task as backup. This is a speculative execution of tasks. It is enabled by default and can be set to false for tasks that take more time, that is, indexing tasks.
`mapred.tasktracker.map.tasks.minimum/` `mapred.tasktracker.reduce.tasks.minimum`	This parameter defines the maximum number of task tracker tasks that can be created. We must understand that having a larger mapper/reducer count compared to physical CPU cores will result in CPU context switching, which may result in an overall slow job completion. However, a balanced per CPU job configuration may result in faster job completion results. Typically, it should be driven based on the number of cores and memory.
`mapred.child.java.opts`	This value can have heap size as a parameter, that is, `Xmx64M`. This value should be driven by the amount of memory and the maximum number of tasks in `tasktracker`.

Chapter 5

Parameter	Description
`mapred.job.map/reduce.memory.mb`	This value sets the virtual memory size for mapper and reducer. Setting this to -1 will use the maximum amount of memory available.
`mapred.jobtracker.maxtasks.per.job`	Defines the maximum number of tasks for a single job. This can be set to -1 to utilize the maximum number of tasks.
`mapred.reduce.parallel.copies`	This defines the number of threads for parallel copy in the reducer task. A very large number can demand more memory and exceed the heap size. This value is driven by network strength. A lower number can help balance the network traffic but slow down the overall transfers. For a gigabit Ethernet, this value can be set between 10 and 15.
`mapreduce.reduce.input.limit`	This value determines the limit on the input size of the reducer. This can be set to -1, that is, no limit.
`mapred.min.split.size`	During execution, map tasks are created for each slice/split. This parameter lets you control the size of each slice. Setting it to 0 enables Hadoop to determine this size.

You can perform additional enhancements in `core-site.xml`:

Parameter	Description
`io.sort.factor`	When heavy output is expected from map jobs (particularly for large jobs), this value should be set to higher values (default is 10). This defines the number of input files that get merged in a batch during the map/reduce task.
`io.sort.mb`	This defines the buffer size in megabytes for sorting. From experience, this value can be approximately 20% to 30% of the child heap size defined using `mapred.child.java.opts`. The default is 100 MB.

Monitoring Solr instance

You can monitor the Solr instance for the purpose of memory and CPU usage. There are various ways of doing this; a simple administration of Solr provides you with some statistics for the usage. Using standard tools like JConsole and JVisualVM, you can connect to the Solr process for monitoring the memory usage, threads, and CPU usage:

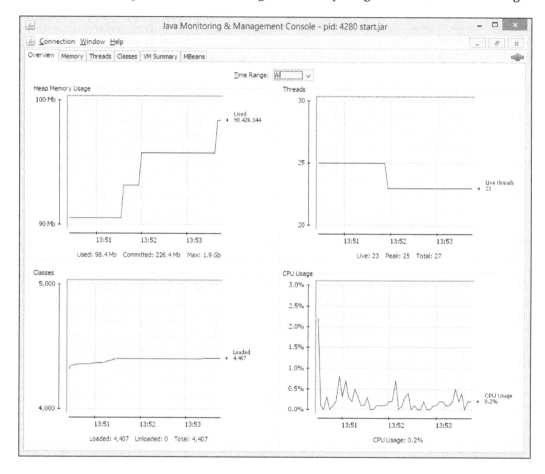

With JConsole, you can also look at different JMX-based MBeans supported by Solr. On an example jetty setup, you can simply connect Solr by using the following procedure:

- Open JDK folder, which is being used by Solr
- Go to the bin folder and run JConsole

Chapter 5

- In JConsole, connect to the Solr process; in case of the default jetty implementation, connect to `start.jar`
- Once connected, switch to the MBean tab

You will find the MBean browser as shown in the following screenshot:

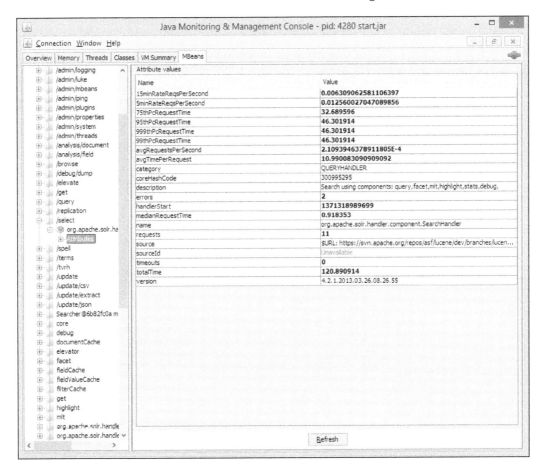

For a clustered search instance, you can connect remotely through JConsole. However, while starting JVM, you need to pass the following parameters to JVM (to bypass authentication and SSL):

```
-Dcom.sun.management.jmxremote.port=<port-no>
-Dcom.sun.management.jmxremote.ssl=false
-Dcom.sun.management.jmxremote.authenticate=false
```

Scaling Search Performance

Using SolrMeter

SolrMeter is a tool that can be used by administrators to access the Solr instance running in a distributed environment to perform stress testing and get the search-related statistics out of it. This tool can be downloaded from `http://code.google.com/p/solrmeter` and it can simply be run by calling:

```
java -jar solrmeter-<version-no>.jar
```

This tool is one of the most powerful tools as it includes both loading and monitoring of your big data search instance. There are four main consoles:

- **Query console**: This shows query-related information such as time taken and queries ran
- **Update Console**: This provides information regarding newly added documents, errors on updates, and so on
- **Commit console**: This provides commit history of documents, time taken, documents for pending commits, and so on
- **Optimize console**: This provides history for optimization, the count of optimize call run, average time taken, errors, and so on, as shown in the following screenshot:

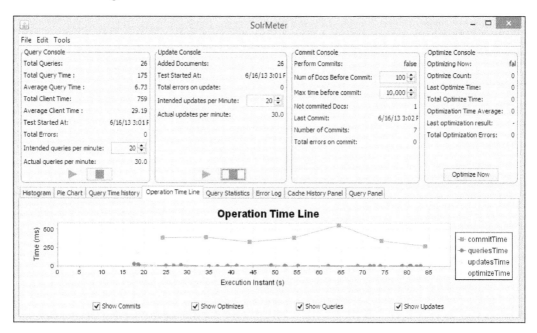

Chapter 5

SolrMeter also displays performance measurements in a graphic manner, that is, histogram, pie chart, query time history, operation timeline, query statistics, errors, and cache history. The charts together provide a detailed view of the query performance. It also provides an option to optimize the indexes by providing a button to optimize now.

Summary

In this chapter, we have covered various ways of optimizing Apache Solr and Hadoop instances. We started by reviewing the schema optimization and optimizing the index. We also looked at optimizing the container, and the search runtime, to speed up the overall process. We reviewed optimizing Hadoop instances. Finally, we looked at different ways of monitoring the Solr instances for performance.

Use Cases for Big Data Search

Many organizations across the globe in different sectors have successfully adapted Apache Hadoop and Solr-based architectures, in order to provide a unique browsing and searching experience for their rapidly growing and diversified information. Let's look at some of the interesting use cases where Big Data Search can be used.

E-Commerce websites

E-Commerce websites are meant to work for different types of users. These users visit the websites for multiple reasons:

- Visitors are looking for something specific, but they find it difficult to describe

- Visitors are looking for a specific price/features of a product

- Visitors come looking for good discounts, to see what's new, and so on

- Visitors wish to compare multiple products on the basis of cost/features/reviews

Most e-commerce websites used to be built on custom developed pages, which ran on a SQL database. Although a database provides excellent capabilities to manage your data structurally, it does not provide high speed searches and facets as it does in Solr. In addition to this, it becomes difficult to keep up with the queries for high performance. As the size of data grows, it hampers the overall speed and user experience.

[133]

Use Cases for Big Data Search

Apache Solr in a distributed scenario provides excellent offerings in terms of a browsing and searching experience. Solr can easily integrate with a database, and provide a high-speed search with real-time indexing. Advanced inbuilt features of Solr, such as suggestions, such as the search, and a spell checker, can effectively help customers gain access to the merchandise they're looking for. Such an instance can easily be integrated with current sites. Faceting can provide interesting filters based on the highest discounts on items, price range, types of merchandise, products from different companies, and so on, which in turn helps to provide a unique shopping experience for end users. Many e-commerce based companies, such as Rakuten.com, DollarDays, and Macy's have acquired distributed Solr-based solutions, preferring these to traditional approaches, so as to provide customers with a better browsing experience.

Log management for banking

Today, many banks in the world are moving towards computerization and using automation in business processes to save costs and improve efficiency. This move requires a bank to build various applications that can support the complex banking use cases. These applications need to interact with each other over standardized communication protocols. A typical enterprise banking sector would consist of software for core banking applications, CMS, credit card management, B2B portals, treasury management, HRMS, ERP, CRM, business warehouses, accounting, BI tools, analytics, custom applications, and various other enterprise applications, all working together to ensure smooth business processes. Each of these applications work with sensitive data: hence, a good banking system landscape often provides high performance and high availability of scalable architecture, along with backup and recovery features, bringing in a completely diversified set of software together, into a secured environment.

Most banks today offer web-based interactions; they not only automate their own business processes, but also access various third-party software of other banks and vendors. A dedicated team of administrators are working 24/7 in order to monitor and handle issues/failures and escalations. A simple application that transfers money from your savings bank account to a loan account may touch upon at least twenty different applications. These systems generate terabytes of data everyday and include transactional data, change logs, and so on.

The problem

The problem arises when any business workflow/transaction fails. With such a complex system, it becomes a big task for system administrators/managers to:

- Find out the issue or the application that has caused the failure
- Try to understand the issue and find out the root cause

- Correlate the issue with other applications
- Keep monitoring the workflow

When multiple applications are involved, the log management across these applications becomes difficult. Some of the applications provide their own administration and monitoring capabilities. However, it make sense to have a consolidated place where everything can be seen at a glance/in one place.

How can it be tackled?

Log management is one of the standard problems where Big Data Search can effectively play a role. Apache Hadoop along with Apache Solr can provide a completely distributed environment to effectively manage the logs of multiple applications, and also provide searching capabilities along with it. Take a look at this representation of a sample log management application user interface:

Use Cases for Big Data Search

This sample UI allows us to have a consolidated log management screen, which may also be transformed into a dashboard to show us the status and the log details. The following reasons explain why Apache Solr and Hadoop-based Big Data Search as the right solution for a given problem:

- The number of logs generated by any banking application are huge in size and are continuous. Most of log-based systems use rotational log management, which cleans up old logs. Given that Apache Hadoop can work on commodity hardware, the overall storage cost for storing these logs becomes cheap, and they can remain in Hadoop storage for a longer time.

- Although Apache Solr is capable of storing any type of schema, common fields, such as log descriptions, levels, and others can be consolidated easily.

- Apache Solr is fast and its efficient searching capabilities can provide different interesting search features, such as highlighting the text or showing snippets of matched results. It also provides a faceted search to drill down and filter results, thereby providing a better browsing experience.

- Apache Solr provides near real-time search capabilities to make the logs immediately searchable, so that administrators can see the latest alarming logs with high severity.

- The cost of building Apache Hadoop with a Solr-based solution provides a low cost alternative infrastructure, which itself is required to have a high speed batch processing of data.

High-level design

The overall design, as shown in the following diagram, can have a schema that contains common attributes across all the log files, such as date and time of the log, severity, application name, user name, type of log, and so on. Other attributes can be added as dynamic text fields:

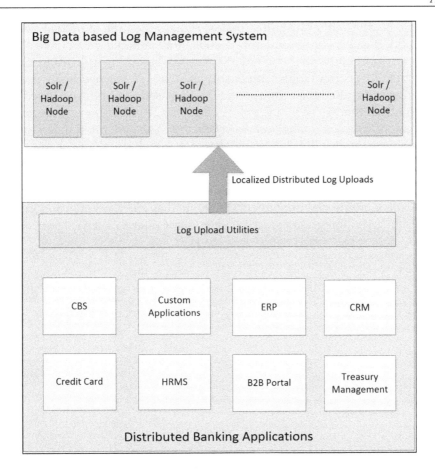

Since each system has a different log schema, these logs have to parsed periodically and then uploaded to a distributed search. The Log Upload Utility or an agent can be a custom script or it can also be based in Apache Kafka, Flume, or even RabbitMQ. Kafka is based on publish-subscribe messaging, and it provides high scalability; you can read more at http://blog.mmlac.com/log-transport-with-apache-kafka/ about how it can be used for log streaming. We need to write script/programs that will understand the log schema, and extract the field data from the logs. Log Upload Utility can feed the outcome to distributed search nodes, which are simply Solr instances running on a distributed system, such as Hadoop. To achieve near real-time search, the Solr configuration requires a change accordingly.

Use Cases for Big Data Search

Indexing can be done either instantly, that is, right at the time of upload, or in a batch operation periodically. The second approach is more suitable if you have a consistent flow of log streams, and also if you have scheduled-based log uploading. Once the log is uploaded in a certain folder, for example `/stage`, a batched index operation using Hadoop's Map-Reduce can generate HDFS-based Solr indexes, based on the many alternatives that we saw in *Chapter 4*, *Big Data Search Using Hadoop and Its Ecosystem*, and *Chapter 5*, *Scaling Search Performance*. The generated index can be read using Solr through a Solr Hadoop connector, which does not use MapReduce capabilities while searching.

Apache Blur is another alternative to indexing and searching on Hadoop using Lucene or Solr. Commercial implementations, such as Hortonworks and LucidWorks provide a Solr-based integrated search on Hadoop (refer to `http://hortonworks.com/hadoop-tutorial/searching-data-solr/`).

Index

A

Analyzer 31
ant build scripting
  URL 98
Apache Ambari 8
Apache Blur
  about 93, 138
  setting up, with Hadoop 94-96
  URL 94
  working, with Hadoop 94
Apache Cassandra
  URL 100
Apache Chukwa 8
Apache Flume 8
Apache Hadoop
  about 2, 6
  configuring 8-14
  core components 4-6
  download link 9
  ecosystem 2-8
  fully distributed setup 9
  HDFS 2
  MapReduce 2
  optimizing 126
  prerequisites 9
  problems 19, 20
  pseudo distributed setup 9
  running 14-16
  single node setup 8
  solutions 19, 20
  ssh, setting up without passphrase 10
  URL 82
Apache HBase 7
Apache HCatalog 8
Apache Hive 7

Apache Ivy
  URL 98
Apache JIRA site
  URL 89
Apache Kafka
  about 137
  URL 137
Apache Lucene core 30
Apache Mahout 7
Apache Oozie 8
Apache Pig 7
Apache Solr
  about 21
  architecture 29-31
  configuring 31
  data, loading 42
  distributed search, enabling with 52
  download link 58
  Hello World 25
  index partitioning 57
  information, querying for 47
  limitations 110
  prerequisites 22
  problems 28, 29
  running, on J2EE containers 25
  running, on jetty 23, 24
  setting up 22
  solutions 28, 29
  working, with Cassandra 96, 97
Apache Sqoop 8
Apache Storm
  about 101
  download link 102
  installing 102, 103
  master node 101
  slave node 101

[**139**]

Solr, scaling through 101
URL 101
worker node 101
Apache Tika 31, 46
Apache ZooKeeper
about 7
URL 60
Application Master (AM) 5
architecture, Solr
about 29
index replicator 30
architecture, SolrCloud 54-57
availability, CAP theorem 82

B

big data
about 1, 2
searching, Katta used 86

C

Cache Autowarming 122
CAP theorem
about 82
URL 72, 82
Cassandra 96, 97
Cassandra integration
about 98
multinode Cassandra, integrating 100
single node configuration 98-100
collection 27, 54
commit
about 115
autocommit 116
soft commit 116
configuration files, Apache Hadoop 11, 12
configuration files, Solr
about 37
instance configuration,
with solrconfig.xml 38-40
other configuration 41
Solr core, working with 38
Solr plugin 40
Solr.xml, working with 38
consistency 82
consoles, SolrMeter
commit console 130

optimize console 130
query console 130
update console 130
core components, Hadoop
about 4-6
Application Master (AM) 5
DataNodes 5
NameNode 5
Node Manager (NM) 5
Resource Manager (RM) 5
SecondaryNameNode 5
cran mirrors
URL 105
curl/wget utilities 43

D

Data Import Handler (DIH) 31
data loading
about 42
data import handlers 43
request handler, extracting 42
rich documents, working with 46
SolrJ, using 44, 45
DataNodes 5
DDL (Data Definition Language) 8
Distributed Deadlock 110
distributed search
about 50
distributed search patterns 50, 51
enabling, Apache Solr used 52
distributed search, with Apache Blur
about 93, 94
Apache Blur, setting up
with Hadoop 94-96
DNS (Domain Name System) 17
document
about 33
routing 68, 69
document cache 124
DocValue 34
DSE
URL 98

E

E-Commerce websites
about 133

usage 133, 134
Elastic Load Balancing
  URL 52
elements, Solr schema
  defaultSearchField 37
  similarity 37
  uniqueKey 37
enterprise distributed search,
      implementation scenarios
  master/slave 51
  multi-nodes 51
  multi-tenant 51
enterprise distributed search, using
    SolrCloud
  building 57
  collections, creating 65, 66
  document, adding to SolrCloud 64
  replicas, creating 65, 66
  shards, creating 65, 66
  SolrCloud, setting up for
      development 58-60
  SolrCloud, setting up for production 60-63
ETL (Extract-Transform-Load) 8
eventual consistency 54

F

fault tolerance, SolrCloud 71, 72
fields, Apache Solr 33
field value cache 124
filter cache 124
Filters 31

G

garbage collection 121
Gartner
  URL 81

H

Hadoop. *See* **Apache Hadoop**
Hadoop cluster
  setting up 17-19
Hadoop Distributed File System (HDFS) 2
Hello World, with Apache Solr
  about 25
  Solr administration 27

Solr navigation 27
HiveQL 7
Hortonworks
  reference link, for data search 138

I

Index Handler 31
index optimization
  about 114
  commit 115
  concurrent clients, optimizing 119
  container, optimizing 119
  indexing buffer size, limiting 115
  index merge, optimizing 117, 118
  Java virtual memory, optimizing 120, 121
  optimize option, for merging index 118
  performing 114
index partitioning 57
Index Reader 30
Index Replicator 30
Index Searcher 30
Index Writer 30
information, Solr
  querying 47

J

J2EE containers
  Solr, running on 25
Java 1.6
  URL 9
JDK
  URL 22
Jetty
  Solr, running on 23
JVM
  URL 29, 119

K

Katta
  about 86
  architecture 86
  indexes, creating 88
  URL 86
  URL, for integrating with Solr 88
  used, for searching big data 86

working 86, 87
Katta cluster
  about 87
  download link, for distribution 87
  setting up 87
  URL, for sample creator script 88
Katta Master 86
K-means clustering
  URL 106

L

laggard problem 110
lazy field loading 125
legacy distributed search
  reference link 52
load balancing, SolrCloud 71
log management, for banking
  about 134
  high-level design 136-138
  problem 134
  resolution 135, 136

M

MapReduce
  about 2
  using 3
map-side indexing 89, 90
Map Task 3
MongoDB
  about 73, 74
  data 74
  installing 75, 76
  Solr indexes, creating from 77-79
  URL 73
  URL, for project repository 77
MongoDB integration
  about 72
  MongoDB 73, 74
  MongoDB, installing 75, 76
  NoSQL 73
  Solr indexes, creating from
      MongoDB 77-79

N

NameNode 5

near-real-time search 116
Node Manager (NM) 5
NoSQL
  about 73, 82
  database 7
  relating, to Big Data 73

P

parallel-ssh
  URL 9
partition tolerance 82
Planet Cassandra
  URL 96
Portable Document Format (PDF) 46
post.jar 26
python
  download link 103

Q

Query Parser 30
query result cache 124

R

R
  about 104
  open source packages 104
  Solr, integrating with 105-107
  URL 104
reduce-side indexing 91-93
Reduce Tasks 3
request handler
  about 41
  extracting 42
  URL 41
Resource Manager (RM) 5
Response Writer 31
Rich Text format (RTF) 46
Round Robin algorithm
  reference link 60

S

search performance
  limits 110
  scaling 109

search runtime optimization
about 121
filter queries 122
Hadoop, optimizing 125-127
optimizing, through search query 122
Solr cache, optimizing 122, 123
search schema optimization
about 111
default search field, specifying 111
search schema fields, configuring 111
stemming 112
stop words 112
SecondaryNameNode 5
Secure shell (ssh) 9
sequential updates 54
shard index or slice, SolrCloud 55
sharding algorithm, SolrCloud
about 68
document routing 68, 69
fault tolerance 72
load balancing 71
shard splitting 70
Shard Leader, SolrCloud 55
shard replica, SolrCloud 55
shards 52
shard splitting, SolrCloud 70
Solandra
URL 98
Solr
about 104
advanced analytics 104
integrating, with R 105-107
scaling, through Storm 101
Solr 5.0
URL 24
Solr 1045 Patch
about 89
using 89, 90
Solr 1301 Patch
about 91
running 92
using 91, 92
Solr cache optimization
about 122, 123
common parameters 123
document cache 124
field value cache 124

filter cache 124
lazy field loading 125
query result cache 124
Solr Cell 42
SolrCloud
architecture 54-57
parameters, for development process 58
problems 66, 67
resolutions 66, 67
used, for building enterprise distributed
search 57
working with 53
ZooKeeper, using 53
Solr configuration
about 31
conf/ folder 32
configuration files 37
data/ folder 32
lib/ folder 32
Solr schema, defining 32
structure 32
solrconfig.xml file
declarations 38, 39
Solr Core 27, 55
Solr folder
contrib/ 23
dist/ 23
docs/ 23
example/ 23
licenses/ 23
Solr HDFS connector
working with 82-85
Solr instance
monitoring 128, 129
monitoring, SolrMeter used 130, 131
SolrJ
about 44
interacting, through 44, 45
SolrMeter
about 130
consoles 130
URL 130
used, for monitoring Solr instance 130
Solr plugin
about 40
filters 41
request handlers 41

[143]

search components 41
Solr schema
defining 32
dynamic fields 34
elements 37
fields, copying 35
field types, dealing with 35
metadata configuration 36
Solr fields 33, 34
Solr Transactional Log 64
STDIN (standard input stream) 43
stemming
about 112
algorithms 112
stop words 112
Storm. *See* **Apache Storm**
sunspot 45

T

technologies, Solr
.NET 46

Java 46
JavaScript 45
Perl 46
PHP 46
Python 46
Ruby 45
Tokenizer 31

Y

YARN (Yet Another Resource Negotiator) 4

Z

Znode 53
ZooKeeper
about 53
download link 102
features 53, 54

Thank you for buying
Scaling Big Data with Hadoop and Solr
Second Edition

About Packt Publishing

Packt, pronounced 'packed', published its first book, *Mastering phpMyAdmin for Effective MySQL Management*, in April 2004, and subsequently continued to specialize in publishing highly focused books on specific technologies and solutions.

Our books and publications share the experiences of your fellow IT professionals in adapting and customizing today's systems, applications, and frameworks. Our solution-based books give you the knowledge and power to customize the software and technologies you're using to get the job done. Packt books are more specific and less general than the IT books you have seen in the past. Our unique business model allows us to bring you more focused information, giving you more of what you need to know, and less of what you don't.

Packt is a modern yet unique publishing company that focuses on producing quality, cutting-edge books for communities of developers, administrators, and newbies alike. For more information, please visit our website at www.packtpub.com.

About Packt Open Source

In 2010, Packt launched two new brands, Packt Open Source and Packt Enterprise, in order to continue its focus on specialization. This book is part of the Packt Open Source brand, home to books published on software built around open source licenses, and offering information to anybody from advanced developers to budding web designers. The Open Source brand also runs Packt's Open Source Royalty Scheme, by which Packt gives a royalty to each open source project about whose software a book is sold.

Writing for Packt

We welcome all inquiries from people who are interested in authoring. Book proposals should be sent to author@packtpub.com. If your book idea is still at an early stage and you would like to discuss it first before writing a formal book proposal, then please contact us; one of our commissioning editors will get in touch with you.

We're not just looking for published authors; if you have strong technical skills but no writing experience, our experienced editors can help you develop a writing career, or simply get some additional reward for your expertise.

Mastering Hadoop

ISBN: 978-1-78398-364-3   Paperback: 374 pages

Go beyond the basics and master the next generation of Hadoop data processing platforms

1. Learn how to optimize Hadoop MapReduce, Pig, and Hive.

2. Dive into YARN and learn how it can integrate Storm with Hadoop.

3. Understand how Hadoop can be deployed on the cloud and gain insights into analytics with Hadoop.

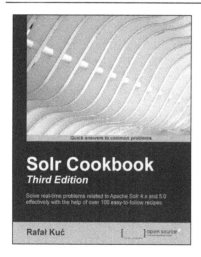

Solr Cookbook
Third Edition

ISBN: 978-1-78355-315-0   Paperback: 356 pages

Solve real-time problems related to Apache Solr 4.x and 5.0 effectively with the help of over 100 easy-to-follow recipes

1. Solve performance, setup, configuration, analysis, and querying problems in no time.

2. Learn to efficiently utilize faceting and grouping.

3. Explore real-life examples of Apache Solr and how to deal with any issues that might arise using this practical guide.

Please check www.PacktPub.com for information on our titles

Building Hadoop Clusters [Video]

ISBN: 978-1-78328-403-0   Duration: 2:34 hours

Deploy multi-node Hadoop clusters to harness the Cloud for storage and large-scale data processing

1. Familiarize yourself with Hadoop and its services, and how to configure them.
2. Deploy compute instances and set up a three-node Hadoop cluster on Amazon.
3. Set up a Linux installation optimized for Hadoop.

Big Data Analytics with R and Hadoop

ISBN: 978-1-78216-328-2   Paperback: 238 pages

Set up an integrated infrastructure of R and Hadoop to turn your data analytics into Big Data analytics

1. Write Hadoop MapReduce within R.
2. Learn data analytics with R and the Hadoop platform.
3. Handle HDFS data within R.
4. Understand Hadoop streaming with R.
5. Encode and enrich datasets into R.

Please check www.PacktPub.com for information on our titles

www.ingramcontent.com/pod-product-compliance
Ingram Content Group UK Ltd.
Pitfield, Milton Keynes, MK11 3LW, UK
UKHW011341050325
4871UKWH00036B/509